# JUST CHURCH

# JUST CHURCH

## Catholic Social Teaching, Synodality, and Women

**Phyllis Zagano**

Paulist Press
New York / Mahwah, NJ

Please note that unless otherwise stated, all papal and Vatican documents can be found online at www.vatican.va.

Library of Congress Cataloging-in-Publication Data available upon request.

ISBN 978-0-8091-5653-5 (paperback)
ISBN 978-0-8091-8814-7 (e-book)

Published by Paulist Press
997 Macarthur Boulevard
Mahwah, New Jersey 07430
www.paulistpress.com

Printed and bound in the
United States of America

*For Irene Kelly, RSHM*

Turning and turning in the widening gyre
The falcon cannot hear the falconer;
Things fall apart; the centre cannot hold;
Mere anarchy is loosed upon the world,
The blood-dimmed tide is loosed, and everywhere
The ceremony of innocence is drowned;
The best lack all conviction, while the worst
Are full of passionate intensity.

Surely some revelation is at hand;
Surely the Second Coming is at hand.
The Second Coming! Hardly are those words out
When a vast image out of *Spiritus Mundi*
Troubles my sight: somewhere in sands of the desert
A shape with lion body and the head of a man,
A gaze blank and pitiless as the sun,
Is moving its slow thighs, while all about it
Reel shadows of the indignant desert birds.
The darkness drops again; but now I know
That twenty centuries of stony sleep
Were vexed to nightmare by a rocking cradle,
And what rough beast, its hour come round at last,
Slouches towards Bethlehem to be born?

William Butler Yeats, "The Second Coming"

# Contents

# Foreword

atholic Social Teaching and synodality, for which Pope Francis has advocated tirelessly, are powerful shaping forces in the life of the contemporary Church. Catholic Social Teaching, whose principles draw directly on Jesus's proclamation and embodiment of God's reign, can form members of the Church for engagement with civil society that is constructive, while also being properly critical of all that damages humanity and the whole of creation. Synodality can foster practices that further the realization of the Church as the people of God, the community of baptized believers who share equally in the gifts of the Holy Spirit and are called together to live as missionary disciples of Jesus Christ. The vision for the ecclesial community that the two dimensions of Catholic life depict is compelling and attractive. Like all visions, however, this one for the Church is vulnerable to more than a few "shadows."

Not least among these shadows is the danger that efforts to translate the vision into practice fail to be as all-encompassing as the vision itself. Phyllis Zagano writes with a clear awareness of this danger, particularly as it applies to the exclusion or marginalization of women in the Church. *Just Church* is a compelling reminder to the Church, at every level and in every setting, that true justice and authentic synodality require the inclusion of *all* the baptized in discerning what constitutes constructive mission in the Church's present moment in history. Most notably, Zagano's work underscores that the Church can be a faithful promoter of justice in the world only if justice reigns in the Church. This justice requires inclusion and generosity rather than discrimination and suspicion. Zagano homes in on the status of women as a test case for the primacy of justice.

In making the case for new practices in the Church—practices that can serve justice—Phyllis Zagano begins with a clear, concise, and accessible overview of both the core principles of Catholic Social Teaching and the dynamics of effective synodality. This background will be enriching for the reflection of individuals in the Church, but perhaps especially for parishes and dioceses as they endeavor to ensure that their ways of proceeding and decision-making do indeed reflect the richness at the heart of the Church's self-understanding. In illustrating the deep roots that a commitment to justice has in the Church's self-understanding, Zagano's writing will encourage those who work to ensure that women and all other members of the Church are able to exercise their share in Christ's prophetic and pastoral offices.

Phyllis Zagano has long been a champion of equality in the Church. In this book, Zagano continues this advocacy, doing so by drawing trajectories from the heart of the Church's proclamation. *Just Church* reminds us that the grace of the Holy Spirit ceaselessly prompts us to act on our convictions. A Church that is responsive to its own proclamation will be more just and more synodal, and so more faithful to grace.

*Richard Lennan*
*Boston College—School of Theology and Ministry*

# Acknowledgments

The question that presented the need for this work came from Paul McMahon, editorial director of Paulist Press. He suggested a fresh and uncomplicated discussion of the central issues the Church faces today. While some of my more popular writing had been collected and published by Garratt Publishing in Australia as *Just Catholic: The Future Is Now* (2021), my newer academic writing more readily suggested this book. It is intended as an accessible work for the people of God, who care and care deeply about the direction of the Church, and who have hope in the future.

At the start, the ongoing process of the Synod on Synodality means there will be no end to the discussion—or to the research. And so, this book is only a beginning. The conversation will continue. As this work goes to press, I recall the many colleagues and friends who have helped me think about the questions here and who, in many cases, helped me find materials. My recollections of conversations by Zoom, telephone, and in person join countless emails filled with information, corrections, and not a few opinions.

With deep gratitude I thank all who have contributed to this work—those named and unnamed.

I am indebted to the current and former journalists and editors who helped, each a generous fact and footnote finder, particularly David Gibson (Fordham University), Christopher Lamb (*The Tablet*),

Joshua McElwee (*National Catholic Reporter*), Bernadette Reis, FSP (Vatican Media), and Cindy Wooden (*Catholic News Service*).

Many of the concepts developed here began as lecture topics, and so I extend thanks to the people who invited me to speak, especially the officers and staff of Voice of the Faithful in Newton, Massachusetts; University of San Diego Harpst Center for Catholic Thought and Culture, California; Emory University Aquinas Center in Atlanta, Georgia; Kings University in London, Ontario, Canada; Margaret Beaufort Institute of Theology, Cambridge (UK); Sacred Heart University in Fairfield, Connecticut; De La Salle University, Manila, Philippines; and of the parishes and other groups who joined the conversation.

The editors of my earlier publications on Catholic Social Teaching, synodality, and women in the Church deserve special thanks: Carlos Frederico Barboza de Souza, editor of *Horizonte* (Brazil); Bruce Bradley, SJ, editor of *Studies* (Dublin); Shaji George Kochuthara, editor of *Asian Horizons* (India); Anthony Towey, editor of *Pastoral Review* (London); Bernard Treacy, OP, Director of Dominican Publications and editor of *Doctrine and Life* (Ireland); and Brendan Walsh, editor of *The Tablet* (England). They join the many editors of the *National Catholic Reporter* and the *Religion News Service* who parsed and published my general essays on these topics.

I am especially indebted to Michael A. Perry, OFM, who kindly explained the new regulations regarding superiors of religious orders and institutes, and to the canon lawyers who helped me better understand both law and terminology, including James Conn, SJ, Fred Easton, Karla Felix-Rivera, Michael Hilbert, SJ, Robert O. Morrissey, and Gerald E. Murray.

My unending gratitude extends to the colleagues, research assistants, and translators who cheerfully assisted me while writing this book, including Denver Beattie, Veronica Brand, RSHM, Brian Butcher, Colleen Gibson, SSJ, Carolyn Osiek, RSCJ, Jacob Rinderknecht, Gina Scaringella, OP, and the many others who helped and encouraged me along the way.

At Hofstra University, technical assistance large and small came my way from the Educational Technology staff, including and especially

Mischa Cuthbert, Sean Donohue, Graham Howe, Nezam Khan, and Alex Smiros; from Alan J. Kelly, Gabrielle McCartin, Terrence M. Moore, and Antoinette Pizarro of the Development and Alumni Affairs staff; from senior secretaries Joanne Herlihy (Department of Religion) and Mary Rose Sinacori (Department of History); and from the librarians and staff of the Axinn Library, especially Wallens Augustin. There were more. It takes a university.

Without question, the generous assistance of the Weigand Family Fund, the National Philanthropic Trust, and many generous private donors assisted greatly in this project.

Joining Paul McMahon at Paulist Press are kind individuals, many of whom I have never met, who brought this book along in record speed and unfailing professionalism. Bob Byrns, Paulist Press's director of marketing and sales, gave patient encouragement all along the way.

As the book rushed toward completion, Donna Ciangio, OP (Archdiocese of Newark), and Claire Shirtzer (St. John's University) provided careful and thoughtful reviews of the manuscript.

Finally, this book is dedicated to my dear friend Irene Kelly, RSHM, who reads everything I write before it appears in print. Besides offering me good cheer and support throughout its composition, her comments and corrections to this work have made it better. To her and all who have encouraged me in my work, I offer my most sincere thanks.

*August 15, 2022*
*Feast of the Assumption*

# Introduction

T wenty centuries of stony sleep? Not really. There are times in the
history of the Church when justice was the order of the day, when
women were well regarded, and when saying "Church" indicated all the
people of God, not the hierarchical few. That situation began to change
during and after the Second Vatican Council, which recommended
a return to synodality including all its members. That restoration
continues along a bumpy road.

Even though *synodality* is the buzzword of the day, the fact
remains that members of the hierarchy are, or at least consider themselves, insulated from the opinions about Church from those members
on the periphery—and the people most cut out of the conversation at
the highest level are women. Perhaps not the women newly named to
positions in the Roman Curia, nor the women chancellors, canon lawyers, or other professionals in diocesan chanceries, nor even the women
theologians, journalists, and activists. However, these all are liable to be
excluded.

Joining them are the poor and the marginalized people, the
women on the periphery for whom no one speaks and, in too many
instances, to whom no one ministers. As they cry out in pain from the
wounds of war, the women on the periphery mourn the rape of the land
and of their sisters. As those in power meet in draped hotel meeting
rooms, heated or air conditioned as the outside temperature dictates,

the poor women on the periphery remain either huddled against the cold or perspiring in the heat. As supermarkets fill with nutritious food-stuff and useless snacks, these poor women on the periphery scrape along to find what they can to eat and drink, hoping that the next day will bring some relief from pain, weather, and hunger.

The periphery, Pope Francis has said, is the center. But as Yeats pointed out, "the center cannot hold."

How can the coming implosion of Church and society be addressed? How can one mind contain the competing challenges of the two sides of society's coin—the rich and the poor; the clerics and the "outsiders"; the politicians and the disenfranchised; the famous and the unknown?

Society has its ills, and the Church attempts to address them. These ills fall into many categories, some neat, others not so neat; some easy to comprehend, others twisted into labyrinthian knots that challenge all perceptions.

And the Church has its own ills. No one needs pounds of synod reports to parse them. The top-heavy structure does not listen to the people, and the people, increasingly, do not listen to the structure. Therein lies the crux of the matter. Women are at the bottom yet, strangely, in the center. Women have been the minsters, silently, efficiently, and professionally keeping that same top-heavy structure afloat.

But the structure seems disconnected from reality *and* from the gospel. The question presents itself: How can the Church be just? How can the Church exist justly within both the world and itself? How can the Catholic Church be one that both espouses justice and be just? Does internal injustice mitigate against any realistic means of speaking to the problems of the world?

Discussions about including the laity in decision-making and about the ordination of women hang over any other considerations. Pope Francis reorganized his Roman Curia following eight years of consultations with his "C-9" group of cardinals, originally one from each continent, and on March 19, 2022, the ninth anniversary of his inauguration as pope, published his apostolic constitution, *Praedicate Evangelium.* The apostolic constitution, originally published only in

Italian, calls the Church and the Curia to "Preach the Gospel" and is explicit in describing the Curia's organization and "its service to the Church and the World."

While *Praedicate Evangelium* promises more lay involvement in governance, exegetes are quick to point to positions they believe require clerical orders. Given that "the laity" is sometimes code for "women," and given the fact that there are distinct levels of discussion relative to the ordination of women (one, as deacons, another as priests), the essential problem remains: How can women be part of the Church in a just manner? How can women be treated justly? Is a "just Church" possible?

Essentially, there are two main categories in the discussion of a "just Church." The two—ecclesiology (theology applied to the Church's organizational structure) and Catholic Social Teaching—are the framework for analyzing the possibilities for "justice" within the Church. Together, they can point to a new reality that describes "Church" as the entire people of God, not simply the hierarchy.

# 1

# Catholic Social Teaching

The discussion of a just Church can become circular. Which comes first? A revised and renewed ecclesiology or the application of Catholic Social Teaching? Given that the issues taken up by recent synods revolve around Catholic Social Teaching, and that within those topics are considerations of significant impact on women, the question of justice can begin there.

To determine whether the Church is just or even if it can meet its own criteria for justice, it is necessary to examine briefly what comprises Catholic Social Teaching. That is, what does the Catholic Church present to the world as requirements for justice in organizations, including (and one might argue especially) in the Church?

## GROWTH AND DEVELOPMENT

Catholic Social Teaching in the modern era begins with Pope Leo XIII's encyclical *Rerum Novarum* (May 15, 1891), "On Capital and

Labor." In it, Leo presents some 14,500 words on the rights and duties of the topic.

Before examining Leo's encyclical, however, it is important to review the various levels of Church documents. Not all address Catholic Social Teaching, and not all have the same authority.

*Apostolic constitutions* are the most solemn of documents issued by popes and become universal or particular law of the Church, depending on how and to whom they are directed.

Next are *encyclicals*. These papal "circular" letters present pastoral advice or opinion. Since 1740, they have been used to explain certain doctrines. *Rerum Novarum*, which presents Catholic Social Teaching on the question of work, and the relation of capital to labor, is such a document.

After papal encyclicals are *motu proprios*, legislative documents issued on the pope's own initiative (*motu proprio* means "on one's own initiative") and are signed by him.

*Apostolic exhortations*, first used by Pope Pius XII in 1939, are addressed to all the faithful and clergy and discuss a specific topic. One example of an apostolic exhortation is John Paul II's *Familiaris Consortio* (November 22, 1981), "On the Role of the Christian Family in the Modern World."

As Catholic Social Teaching has evolved since the turn of the twentieth century, many papal documents have further elucidated and expanded its concepts. Essentially, all reflect how the gospel applies to contemporary situations in the modern world.

Not all scholars agree with all the documents, and there is a marked change in their tone following the close of the Second Vatican Council (October 1962 to December 1965). It was Vatican II that sowed the seeds of synodality that have sprouted during the pontificate of Francis, stunningly represented by his efforts to have the entire Church participate in a "Synod on Synodality," which opened in September 2021. These worldwide synodal discussions, aimed for an initial October 2023 meeting in Rome, have taken place against the backdrop of Catholic Social Teachings, including the many issues related *at what point are there too many cooks in the kitchen?*

to women described in prior papal and synodal documents. Unfortunately, many dioceses in many countries did not participate, or did not participate fully, in the synodal process, thereby eliminating the voices, ideas, hopes, and dreams of many persons and thereby rebuking Vatican II.

In addition to *Rerum Novarum*, the foundational documents of Catholic Social Teaching prior to Vatican II include Pope Pius XI's *Quadragesimo Anno* (May 15, 1931) and Pope John XXIII's *Mater et Magistra* (May 15, 1961) and *Pacem in Terris* (April 11, 1963). Interestingly, only the encyclicals of the twentieth century are addressed to both clergy and the laity. *Rerum Novarum* is addressed "To Our Venerable Brethren the Patriarchs, Primates, Archbishops, Bishops, and Other Ordinaries of Places Having Peace and Communion with the Apostolic See."

Vatican II documents include *Gaudium et Spes*, the Pastoral Constitution on the Church in the Modern World, and *Dignitatis Humanae*, the council's declaration on religious freedom, each promulgated by Pope Paul VI, December 7, 1965. Three additional documents signed by Paul VI expand social justice themes explored by the council: his encyclical *Populorum Progressio* (March 26, 1967), his apostolic letter *Octogesima Adveniens* (May 14, 1971), celebrating the eightieth anniversary of *Rerum Novarum*, and his apostolic exhortation *Evangelii Nuntiandi* (December 8, 1975) on the "fundamental commitment" to preach the gospel. Together, they form much of the engine driving the uneven reception of the Second Vatican Council.

Various documents from the pontificates of John Paul II, Benedict XVI, and Francis build on the traditions of Catholic Social Teaching (see Appendix I), and some lead to a new ecclesiology, a new way of being Church.

In many respects, the new way of being Church is the old way of being Church. Over the centuries, centralization has encrusted the possibilities of all Church members having a voice. While all Church members are called to accede to doctrinal teachings, fewer are charged with analyzing their development, to the point that many argue that doctrine cannot develop at all.

So, despite the hopeful titles of documents, the Church has been stymied for centuries in its hopes to address and understand the *rerum novarum* of the modern age.

This is not to argue for modernism as the Church denies it. Scholars of the early twentieth century wrote about the ways the world changed in response to "modernity," specifically the changes brought about by industrialization. The prevalent view was that, in many respects, all modernization marked a human progress that moved toward a universal utopia.

Within Catholicism, individuals wrote how Catholicism could be reconciled with the changes of society. They specifically supported historical-critical methods of renewing understandings of Scripture and Tradition. These, along with the emerging philosophies of the times, caused great discussion inside and outside the Church, predominantly in Europe and North America. The kernel of the controversy is the fact that objective truth is always received subjectively. The turn to the subject—the subjective reevaluation of truth—in and of itself encouraged introspective analysis of religious experience, which, in turn, could call some Church pronouncements into question.

In 1910, Pope Saint Pius X sought to slow the development of these beliefs within the Church with his *motu proprio, Sacrorum Antistitum*,[1] explaining his institution of laws against modernism and requiring all clergy, religious superiors, officials of the Roman Curia, and seminary professors to affirm the Oath against Modernism. The Oath basically charges that modern development cannot replace revelation, specifically professing that God can be known as the cause of all creation, that attested miracles and prophecies verified the divine origin of Christianity, and that the Church was instituted by Christ and is maintained by his successors. Finally, the Oath requires assent to the unchanging nature of "the doctrine of the faith."

The Oath thereby appears to reject the notion of the development of doctrine, and includes submission to Pope Pius X's encyclical *Pascendi Dominci Gregis* (1907), "On the Doctrine of the Modernists,"[2] and the decree of the Holy Office *Lamentabili Sane*, "Syllabus Condemning the Errors of the Modernists."[3] In relation to the history of dogmas, *Lamentabili Sane* lists sixty-five beliefs that Church members must deny, each rooted in determinations made through the evaluation of Scripture. For example, no. 53 states, "The organic constitution of the Church is not immutable. Like human society, Christian society is subject to a perpetual evolution." In other words, the Church as it is not subject to development and therefore cannot change. The Oath concludes,

> Finally, I declare that I am completely opposed to the error of the modernists who hold that there is nothing divine in sacred tradition; or what is far worse, say that there is, but in a pantheistic sense, with the result that there would remain nothing but this plain simple fact-one to be put on a par with the ordinary facts of history-the fact, namely, that a group of men by their own labor, skill, and talent have continued through subsequent ages a school begun by Christ and his apostles. I firmly hold, then, and shall hold to my dying breath the belief of the Fathers in the charism of truth, which certainly is, was, and always will be in the succession of the episcopacy from the apostles. The purpose of this is, then, not that dogma may be tailored according to what seems better and more suited to the culture of each age; rather, that the absolute and immutable truth preached by the apostles from the beginning may never be believed to be different, may never be understood in any other way.

Clearly, modernism questioned the Neo-Scholasticism of Pius X's predecessor, Leo XIII. If we are to consider Catholic Social Teaching as it applies to the internal structures and functions of the Church, we cannot avoid looking over our shoulders at the anti-intellectualism that spawned Pius X's encyclical *Pascendi Dominci Gregi* and the decree of the Holy Office *Lamentabili Sane*, which culminated in the Oath against Modernism.

# APPLICATION

Against this backdrop of the intellectual battles at the dawn of the modern age, we can review the application of Catholic Social Teaching in our own age. There are seven generally acknowledged themes in Catholic Social Teaching that can be gleaned from its growth and development: (1) Dignity of Work and Rights of Workers; (2) Life and Dignity of the Human Person; (3) Solidarity; (4) Care for God's Creation; 5) Call to Family, Community, and Participation; (6) Option for the Poor and Vulnerable; and (7) Rights and Responsibilities. Some cross over to questions of ecclesiology, and it is possible for each to be applied internally to the structural accommodations of the Church as an organization created to spread the teachings of the gospel. Some can be recognized as criticisms of the ways and means the hierarchical Church has used and uses as it has veered toward clericalism.

*[handwritten margin note: what is meant by apply internally?]*

## Dignity of Work and Rights of Workers

In the late nineteenth century, toward the end of the Victorian Age, slavery had been abolished in much of the West, and the burgeoning Industrial Revolution created opportunities for profit as cities became more crowded. Most of the developing world, especially South and Southeast Asia and great swaths of Africa, was under colonial rule. *Rerum Novarum* begins by implicitly criticizing the economics of this age. It immediately defends the poorest in class structure at the time:

> That the spirit of revolutionary change, which has long been disturbing the nations of the world, should have passed beyond the sphere of politics and made its influence felt in the cognate sphere of practical economics is not surprising. The elements of the conflict now raging are unmistakable, in the vast expansion of industrial pursuits and the marvellous discoveries of science; in the changed relations between masters and workmen; in the enormous fortunes of some few individuals, and the utter poverty of

the masses; the increased self-reliance and closer mutual combination of the working classes; as also, finally, in the prevailing moral degeneracy. The momentous gravity of the state of things now obtaining fills every mind with painful apprehension; wise men are discussing it; practical men are proposing schemes; popular meetings, legislatures, and rulers of nations are all busied with it—actually there is no question which has taken deeper hold on the public mind.

Therefore, venerable brethren, as on former occasions when it seemed opportune to refute false teaching, We have addressed you in the interests of the Church and of the common weal, and have issued letters bearing on political power, human liberty, the Christian constitution of the State, and like matters, so have We thought it expedient now to speak on the condition of the working classes.[4]

Leo then describes and criticizes the ways of the Industrial Revolution of the prior 100 to 150 years.

The dichotomy of views of the relationships between capital and labor has not changed. In 1854, Charles Dickens's *Hard Times* presented a Coketown (actually, Preston, Lancashire, England) that gave witness to the human toll and sufferings incurred during the Industrial Revolution. The metaphorical hamster wheel of drudgery and misery exemplified the ways labor would, could, and was abused at the time. Others, then and now, defend industrialization and the modernization of work as the single most effective means to raise the populace's standard of living.

Leo was interested in securing the rights of workers, the poor and very poor, for whom subsistence living on the land was replaced by subsistence living in improper and unsafe workplace conditions complicated by abusive employment policies. The dates of Church documents are often informative: *Rerum Novarum* is dated May 15, 1891, the feast day for Saint Isidore the Laborer (San Isidro Labrador, ca. 1070–1130), the Spanish farmworker known for kindness to the poor and to animals. Isidore is credited with several miracles, including other people having seen angels doing his farm plowing with or for him, and his cooked food multiplying to feed the hungry poor. In 1212, when flooding exhumed several cadavers from the Madrid cemetery where he was buried, his body was found incorrupt.[5] Saint Isidore is specifically honored as an example of the dignity of work.

The roots of Catholic Social Teaching extend far deeper than the late nineteenth century, but to pick up its threads there and begin to apply them to the plight of all women—Catholic and non-Catholic—is the aim of this book. All women are impacted by the need for respect of the rights of workers, whether within the context of their own work or that of their husbands and other family members. No matter who is maltreated or disrespected, the pain inflicted by unjust acts or conditions always wounds women.

If the Church is to apply its own teachings to itself, we must assert that the Church must be a fair employer.

## Life and Dignity of the Human Person

It can seem simplistic to say that the life and dignity of people within the Church begins with baptism and must be respected. But when the Church makes statements that imply or directly state that women cannot image Christ, the Risen Lord, there is much to be criticized.

While it may seem incomprehensible in current times to say that women cannot—do not—image Christ, this is the bedrock of the argument that women cannot receive sacramental ordination. The implications of this statement or belief are enormous. Its errors are equally enormous.

To begin with, men and women are ontologically equal. That is, all human beings, all persons, are equal before God. Because they are equal—male *and* female—one cannot be subordinated to the other. While history is rife with heretical statements of ontological subordination, their existence and expulsion from Church teaching supports the essential point that men and women, while not the same, are equal.

Even so, there is significant writing that allows for ontological equality while also admitting hierarchical subordination. Can we admit that societal norms influenced the patristic writers who allowed that wives ought to submit to their husbands? John Chrysostom writes, "Let us take as our fundamental position then that the husband occupies the place of the 'head' and the wife the place of the 'body'" (*Homily XX* on *Ephesians*). Can we allow that he and other Church fathers who found the support for the subordination of women in the writings of Saint Paul were unable to discard the incomplete anthropology of Paul's own time (see Eph 5:22–32)?

*No.*

That is, the ordinary subordination within relationships (mother-son, employer-employee, bishop-presbyter) can transfer to a distorted view of the human person, such that the woman is always considered subordinate to the man, independent of the circumstances of their relationship(s).

To be clear, there is a need for "subordination" in any organization, at least on the managerial level. And there must be an accommodation within families such that decisions can be made. But the ordinary ways of relating that include subordination need not, in fact, *cannot* deny the full humanity of any individual. That is, in all situations, women are not automatically subordinate to men, and women are specifically not automatically subordinate to men based on some notion of their lesser humanity.

We cannot forget that "God created humankind in his image... male and female he created them" (Gen 1:27). The *imago dei* implies, in fact, *requires*, a single-nature anthropology that recognizes male and female persons existing equally. Even canon law allows for this fact with the first canon in the section describing the rights and duties of the Christian faithful:

> From their rebirth in Christ, there exists among all the Christian faithful a true equality regarding dignity and action by which they all cooperate in the building up of the Body of Christ according to each one's own condition and function. (Can. 208)

*What is feminist theology? How far does it go?*

Unfortunately, some might consider "one's own condition and function" as an opening to admitting a dual nature anthropology, but examinations of this and earlier canons (specifically, canon 204) clearly indicate that one's "condition" implies one's relationship to the Church, as baptized or not, as in communion with the Catholic Church or not, as cleric or lay, secular or religious. One's "condition" does not and cannot imply male or female gender. Canon 208, rooted as it is in *Lumen Gentium*, the Second Vatican Council's Dogmatic Constitution on the Church (November 21, 1964), supports single-nature anthropology. *Lumen Gentium* clarifies and expands the concept of equality of the sexes:

> By divine institution Holy Church is ordered and governed with a wonderful diversity. "For just as in one body we have many members, yet all the members have not the same function, so we, the many, are one body in Christ, but severally members one of another." Therefore, the chosen People of God is one: "one Lord, one faith, one baptism"; sharing a common dignity as members from their regeneration in Christ, having the same filial grace and the same vocation to perfection; possessing in common one salvation, one hope and one undivided charity. There is, therefore, in Christ and in the Church no inequality on the basis of race or nationality, social condition or sex, because "there is neither Jew nor Greek: there is neither bond nor free: there is neither male nor female. For you are all 'one' in Christ Jesus."[6]

Certainly, all can agree that "all the members have not the same function." Such would be a destruction of society and especially of the society of Church. But, equally so, "in the Church no inequality on the basis of race or nationality, social condition or sex...." As *Lumen Gentium* points out, restrictions to equal humanity cannot be based on "male nor female."

The Church preaches these facts, but does the Church present them adequately to the world? Evangelization is both an internal and *i do think a barrier exists* ←

external task, and if the Church cannot overcome the perception that it somehow certifies an inequality in the humanness of women in relation to men, evangelization will continue to suffer.

## Solidarity

Solidarity as a principle of Catholic Social Teaching echoes the name of the Independent Self-Governing Trade Union "Solidarity" movement that was founded at the Lenin Shipyard in Gdańsk, Poland, in August 1980, which by September 1981 represented ten million workers. Its activities developed into widespread calls for change and popular opposition to the communist regimes in Eastern Europe, including the Baltic States and parts of ancient Kievan Rus'—Belarus and Ukraine. By 1989, its founder, Lech Wałęsa, was elected president of Poland, ushering in its liberal capitalism in the 1990s.

One hundred years after the promulgation of Leo XIII's *Rerum Novarum*, Pope John Paul II promulgated his encyclical *Centesimus Annus* (May 1, 1991), reinforcing the Church's position on the relationship between capital and labor. In it, the Polish pope addressed the role of the free market, the action of the state, the role of intermediate bodies, and developed principles regarding personal savings and consumer goods. Examining globalization of the markets and the international financial system, he addressed the role of international governments and what is now termed an integral development in solidarity that presented the need for international and cultural formation.

How could this happen? How, in effect, can the gospel be applied to international trade and monetary policy? How could the Church, then one hundred years after the promulgation of *Rerum Novarum*, apply the principals of solidarity to the world? How can the Church today, more than three decades after *Centesimus Annus*, understand its ability and responsibility to address inequalities caused by abusive labor practices and unequal access to capital and goods among the people of the world? Is the Church capable of convincing the world of the need for solidarity—the bedrock of interpersonal, intergovernmental, and interchurch relationships?

And finally, amid all these concerns, how can women be part of the solution, especially given that they are so often damaged by the root of the problems?

In his densely researched book *Cathonomics: How Catholic Tradition Can Create a More Just Economy*, economist Anthony M. Annett reminds the reader that Catholic Social Teaching, particularly in the realm of economics, did not appear on the world stage only with the publication of *Rerum Novarum*.

Annett locates the beginnings of Catholic Social Teaching in Scripture, especially in Jesus's thirty-one parables, in the writings of Church fathers of the patristic era, and in Aristotle and Thomas Aquinas. All spoke to many of the same difficulties the world suffers today.

The writings of the Church fathers show the trajectory of thought on the topic of distribution of wealth and resources. Annett cites Saint Ambrose (ca. 339–97), who was made bishop of Milan by popular acclamation in 374: "The earth belongs to everyone, not to the rich." He reminds his readers of the words of Saint John Chrysostom (ca. 347–407), archbishop of Constantinople, who died in exile: "Not to share our wealth with the poor is theft from the poor," and of the admonition of Saint Cyril of Alexandria (ca. 376–444), patriarch of Alexandria from 412 until his death: "Let us not usurp for ourselves what has been given to us for our brothers and sisters."[7]

Ambrose's admonition can be applied to natural resources —land, water, and the necessary responsible respect for air. Chrysostom's comment, when recalled today, echoes the cries for a fair distribution of wealth with the clear implication that uneven tax structures deeply injure the poor. And Cyril's fifth-century cry on behalf of the poor speaks to those who cause women to barter their bodies and their lives to feed themselves and their children. Whether on the micro or the macro level, any refusal to honor the principals of solidarity injure those least able to sustain the blow, and their injury redounds to a weakening of the fabric of society.

Annett concludes his study with a modern example. As the world continued to suffer the economic and social damages wrought by the

COVID-19 pandemic, he notes the response to its effects is marked generally by a lack of solidarity. Mixed responses from both the private and public sector, complicated then and now by the minority for whom the common good does not override their so-called personal freedoms, often presented as decisions of conscience as regards various public health measures. These included refusals to wear masks and to accept approved inoculations, the ignoring of "lockdown" restrictions, and the spreading of incorrect information, which, in turn, supported a warped notion of freedom and conscience.[8]

Annett presents the responses as outgrowths of modern libertarianism, which seeks to emphasize freedom and autonomy, often at the expense of others. Within the context of American politics since the mid-twentieth century, what can be termed "right-libertarianism" is the antithesis of solidarity. In the economic sphere, he proposes that "the lesson is that protecting people from the excesses of the free market through the power of government institutions is essential for economic and social stability—and even for democracy and peace."[9]

Efforts to promote, even explain, principles of solidarity begin and end with the concept that not only the Church, but the entire world is one family. Further, within the Church solidarity recognizes (or should recognize) that all its members are equal partners in the task of evangelization. That is, individuals are called to recognize their own personal responsibility toward the common good.

## Care for God's Creation

The common good recognizes our common home. Whether in the words of Ambrose, "The earth belongs to everyone, not to the rich," or as elucidated in Pope Francis's encyclical *Laudato Si'* (May 24, 2015), the Christian environmental discussion is gospel centered.

*Laudato Si',* the first words Saint Francis of Assisi (ca. 1181–1226) speaks praising the Lord in his Canticle of Creation, are also Pope Francis's opening words of his encyclical addressing the questions of the modern world's relation to the physical realities of earth, air, and water: "Praise be to you, my Lord, through our Sister, Mother Earth, who sustains and governs us, and who produces various fruit with coloured flowers and herbs."[10] And at the outset, the pope issues a strong wake-up call:

> This sister now cries out to us because of the harm we have inflicted on her by our irresponsible use and abuse of the goods with which God has endowed her. We have come to see ourselves as her lords and masters, entitled to plunder her at will. The violence present in our hearts, wounded by sin, is also reflected in the symptoms of sickness evident in the soil, in the water, in the air and in all forms of life. This is why the earth herself, burdened and laid waste, is among the most abandoned and maltreated of our poor; she "groans in travail" (*Rom* 8:22). We have forgotten that we ourselves are dust of the earth (cf. *Gen* 2:7); our very bodies are made up of her elements, we breathe her air and we receive life and refreshment from her waters.

*Laudato Si'* appeared in 2015. Years later, the earth still suffers, its wounds now compounded by the evils of war, and there is little change and only insignificant efforts to stop the ravage of the planet. Too often, the multifold causes of climate change and environmental devastation are reduced to questions of financial gain. The solution some propose is to recognize that economic growth is essentially stymied by one or another destructive practice.

It can seem odious to depend on the recommendations for financial gain to curb destruction of the planet and its people, but beyond the public relations spin that can be put on some of these efforts, there is at least a small glimmer of hope. For example, the international consulting firm Deloitte Touche Tohmatsu Limited, known as Deloitte and headquartered in London, England, has some 28,000 employees and has commented on climate change, calling it an economic growth imperative. The hope, or assumption, is that economic growth will benefit all.

so too the otherside

For example, Deloitte's January 2022 report, "The Turning Point: A New Economic Climate in the United States," begins by pointing out that the global pandemic seems to have taken the focus off climate catastrophes within the United States, noting California wildfires, Western droughts, hurricanes in the South and Northeast, and the devastating heatwaves in the Pacific Northwest. The report states that over the prior fifty years, the United States alone "suffered a total $1.4 trillion in economic losses due to weather, climate and water hazards"[11] and notes twenty separate billion-dollar weather and climate disasters during 2021 alone.[12] The report goes on to indicate the dangers presented by climate change to various regions of the United States, threatening agriculture and fostering disease, pointing out that rising average temperatures threaten urban and rural infrastructures and, more importantly, workers.

Analysis of current and projected conditions and consequences in the United States are echoed worldwide. The Earth, as Pope Francis reminds us, is our common home. So, the fact that the combined land and ocean temperatures have increased at an average rate of 0.13 degrees Fahrenheit (0.08 degrees Celsius) every ten years since 1880 is alarming enough, but the fact that the average rate of increase since 1981 is more than double points to what people have done to the planet.[13]

Since former U.S. Vice President Al Gore spoke out in the cinematic presentation *An Inconvenient Truth* (2006), the damage to our "common home" has continued, in many respects unabated. Despite international agreements, especially the Paris Agreement, which went into force on November 2, 2016, global warming continues at its average rate. In fact, the Paris Agreement to limit global warming to below 2.0 degrees Celsius may curb the problem, but efforts to reverse the warming trend to preindustrialization rates, that is, to 1.5 degrees Celsius, would benefit every country in the world. As with all international agreements, there is criticism of the methods used by and the intent of signatory parties, but it is an important start.[14]

On local levels, there is much that the Church—as in parishes and dioceses—can do to support initiatives to help heal the planet. Can we consider, for example, how water is used by Church organizations?

Can managers of church buildings review policies regarding decorative plantings? Can they incorporate solar heating and electric panels? In some countries, Church organizations already employ many methods to minimize their negative impacts on the environment. In other countries, they do not seem to take the environmental crisis seriously.

When the Church asks the world to understand the problems of the planet, the people of God have the right and the duty to insist that the parish, the diocese, indeed any Church organizational structure participates in its care.

*(margin note: integrity → agree)*

## Call to Family, Community, and Participation

The concentric circles in which all persons find themselves, moving outward from the self to the family, to the society through work, school, parish, or other community and civic constructs create participation in society. Multiple documents emanating from the Vatican argue on behalf of the family and the sacredness of human life.

Many writers choose one or another of the basic tenets of this portion of Catholic Social Teaching to criticize members of the Church or society, in general. Often, "family" is used to define some persons out of the mix, even out of Christian membership.

Pope Francis has opened the categories in many ways. His post-synodal apostolic exhortation *Amoris Laetitia* (March 19, 2016) responds to two synods on the family, the third Extraordinary General Assembly of the Synod of Bishops on the Family (2014) and the XIV Ordinary General Assembly of the Synod of Bishops on the Family (2015). While later sections of this book will examine these events, in general, and *Amoris Laetitia*, in particular, it is important to note here that misinterpretations of *Amoris Laetitia* and even of synod interventions have wrought division in specific areas of the Church on specific topics, despite there being no change in doctrine presented or predicted.

On the surface, it seems that Church teaching eliminates from membership persons who are in what it terms "irregular" (i.e., not

Church-sanctioned) unions, who are using birth control, who have suffered an abortion, or who affirm distinctive beliefs regarding sex and gender. It cannot be maintained that Francis has annulled any teaching. Rather, it appears that his view is that all the baptized are members of the Church—in one way or another—and that it is the duty of all to attempt to understand and, in some cases forgive, transgressions and differences. → to what extent do we bystand?

The important aspect of Catholic Social Teaching to be emphasized here is that of membership and participation, and hence, the 2021–2023 Synod on Synodality that Francis initiated in the fall of 2021. If all are members, all have the right (and duty) to participate. In fact, as already noted, the Code of Canon Law, in its reflection on doctrinal teaching, states that "there exists among all the Christian faithful a true equality" (Can. 208).

The word *equality* can cause division. The tragedy of clericalism, where certain clerics believe themselves rulers rather than fellow disciples of Christ, creates a tension in all discussion of family, community, and participation. Clericalism overtakes any possibility of true participation, and rigid clericalism overtakes any possibility of discussion about family and community.

The obvious topics of division within the Church begin with abortion, now generally legal on request in most of the Northern Hemisphere, and in Argentina, Australia, Cambodia, China, Colombia, Guyana, Ethiopia, India, Mozambique, New Zealand, Thailand, South Africa, Vietnam, Uruguay, and Zambia. Other countries and jurisdictions join the list regularly. Because the 1973 U.S. Supreme Court decision in *Roe v. Wade* allowing abortion nationwide has been overturned, the question now resides in individual states, resulting in a growing patchwork of laws.[15]

The political conversation in the United States has turned the issue into one that creates a barrier to receiving Communion for Catholic politicians, while at the same time giving a pass to non-Catholics. The problem became particularly relevant with the election of Joseph R. Biden, a Catholic, as president. In 1982, Biden, a long-time U.S. senator and former two-term vice president, voted for a constitutional amendment to allow states to individually overturn *Roe v. Wade*.[16] Since then, his views on abortion policy have evolved. He responded to the June 2022 overturning of *Roe v. Wade* by signing various executive orders aimed at assisting women to navigate the various state laws that then went into effect.

Here, two points are relevant: first, the role of the executive branch is to enforce the law; second, decisions about worthiness for receiving Holy Communion are to be left to the individual and his or her confessor or, in the case of a public figure, the bishop of his place of residence. For the present, Cardinal Wilton D. Gregory, archbishop of Washington, has stated that he will not refuse administering Communion to Biden.

That should have ended criticism by other U.S. bishops. In San Francisco, Archbishop Salvatore J. Cordileone joined the fray by publicly announcing that he had banned then-Speaker of the U.S. House of Representatives, Nancy Pelosi, from receiving Communion, a ban that seems to be in effect only within his archdiocese. Cordileone did garner some support from other diocesan bishops.[17] While pundits and others are free to comment, and indeed there is need for antiabortion writing and rhetoric, it is not the place of an individual bishop who is not the diocesan bishop of the person in question to make a statement overriding that person's bishop.

Other points regarding "participation" converge similarly at the communion rail: birth control, marriage, and questions regarding sexuality and gender. When the Church argues on behalf of the family, it should consider all types of families and care for them.

Chemical and mechanical means of birth control, outlawed by Pope Paul VI's encyclical *Humanae Vitae* (July 25, 1968), found their ways into Catholic homes before, during, and since the pope's letter, which ignored findings and recommendations of the Pontifical Commission on Birth Control, and have most recently come under renewed scrutiny by the Pontifical Academy of Science.

During its term, the Pontifical Commission on Birth Control grew from six European nontheologians appointed in 1963 by John XXIII to an eventual seventy-two members from five continents, including sixteen theologians and an executive committee of sixteen bishops (seven of whom were cardinals). Concluding its work under Paul VI in 1966, the commission's report stated that artificial birth control was not intrinsically evil and individual couples should determine how they might responsibly limit births.[18] A minority report supported Church teaching,[19] and discussion of the matter argued that Paul VI was bound by Pius XI's encyclical *Casti Connubii* (December 31, 1930), which prohibited any form of artificial birth control in an apparent response to the determinations of the 1930 Anglican Lambeth Conference.[20] No matter the rulings, most Catholic women ignore them.

Questions about marriage, sexuality, and gender are equally fraught with contention and clouded with commentary. When framed in the context of "women's rights," they join the logic that argues for unrestricted access to abortion and birth control. When viewed pastorally, they highlight the ways abortion and birth control are defenses against abuse of women. Women are, in fact, protected by Church restrictions against abortion; too many are forced to contracept or abort by their male partners and it is not beyond the realm of possibility that the state could force abortions (e.g., efforts in China to limit births from 1980 to 2016) or act to sterilize women. see pg. 9

Women are protected to some degree by Catholic marriage laws, and when they are abandoned or initially misled, they can remarry. Without doubt, footnote 351 in *Amoris Laetitia* has been misinterpreted and misunderstood by individuals on both sides of the discussion. Suffice it to say here that a bishop can formally dissolve a marriage where ordinary means for annulment are impossible.

The difficult questions related to same-sex relationships and transgender people will not be resolved soon, here or elsewhere. However, the Church does pay attention to science, and if science supports biological reasons for same-sex attraction, even to the point of individuals presenting for medical intervention to support their needs, the Church will have to decide if it can change. NO.

But in each of these situations, the points of respecting families, respecting membership in community (including the Church community) and allowing participation are supported by the basics of Catholic

Social Teaching, which does not seek to exclude, indeed, to ostracize, anyone.

## Option for the Poor and Vulnerable

Who are "the poor" and what does the "preferential option for the poor" mean? Catholic Social Teaching in general and regional synods in particular repeatedly have emphasized the need for the care and recognition of the poor and the vulnerable in society.

The term *preferential option for the poor* was initially presented and adopted in 1968 at the Second Episcopal Conference of Latin America (CELAM) at Medellín, Colombia. It is rooted in the teachings of Jesus and is threaded throughout Catholic Social Teaching. Its reception has been mixed, but the bishops attending the CELAM meeting made a distinct effort to include the excluded poor in their determinations. That is, they approved base communities, the small rural and generally priestless gatherings of Catholics and asked for ways to free the people of God from what they termed the "institutionalized" violence of poverty.

When in May 2002 the Fifth Latin American Episcopal Conference met in Aparecida, Brazil, the drafters included considerations about environmental challenges along with the "preferential option for the poor" that had become part of the core opposition to environmental abuses endangering the livelihoods of so many in the region. Undoubtably, strip mining, clear cutting, and air and water pollution all contributed to the poorest in Central and South America, especially indigenous persons, fleeing their destroyed habitats. In some places, they could no longer grow food or find clean water. Too often, these displaced persons migrated to cities, where the combination of deficient social services and minimal employment prospects endangered their lives. Often, these people were women.

At the time, then-Cardinal Jorge Mario Bergoglio, archbishop of Buenos Aires, was on the Fifth CELAM meeting's document drafting committee. Pope Francis's *Evangelii Gaudium* (2013), *Laudato Si'* (2015), and *Amoris Laetitia* (2016) all refer to or borrow from the document. Francis has continued to speak widely and forcefully on behalf of the poor, and his response to the Final Document of the Amazon Synod (2019) specifically points to the poverty of and violence against women.

Throughout Catholic Social Teaching, the needs of the poor and vulnerable—the *anawim* of the world—are to be recognized. This is a given, presented in Scripture and repeatedly well-acknowledged in many documents. Clearly, the care of the poor is directed throughout Scripture. In the early Eastern Church, the monastic *diaconia* of sharing with the poor is well known and is complemented in the West, as recalled by Pope Benedict XVI in his first encyclical, *Deus Caritas Est*. Benedict reflects on the institutionalization of charity by the Church:

> Towards the middle of the fourth century we see the development in Egypt of the "*diaconia*": the institution within each monastery responsible for all works of relief, that is to say, for the service of charity. By the sixth century this institution had evolved into a corporation with full juridical standing, which the civil authorities themselves entrusted with part of the grain for public distribution. In Egypt not only each monastery, but each individual Diocese eventually had its own *diaconia*; this institution then developed in both East and West. Pope Gregory the Great (+ 604) mentions the *diaconia* of Naples, while in Rome the *diaconiae* are documented from the seventh and eighth centuries. But charitable activity on behalf of the poor and suffering was naturally an essential part of the Church of Rome from the very beginning, based on the principles of Christian life given in the *Acts of the Apostles*. It found a vivid expression in the case of the deacon Lawrence (+ 258).[21]

Benedict then recounts Lawrence's story as told by Saint Ambrose (ca. 339–ca. 397):

Lawrence, responsible for the care of the poor in Rome, was directed by civil authorities to collect and hand over the treasures of the Church. He presented the poor to them, as the true treasures of the Church.[22]

Often overlooked in the recounting of Lawrence's actions, which led to his martyrdom, is that he first collected the Church's riches and gave them to the poor, presumably the same poor whom he presented to the authorities. But we ask again: Who are the poor?

We can applaud the efforts of popes, national episcopal conferences, individual bishops, scholars, and writers, as well as the efforts of various organizations to highlight the detrimental effects of corporate avarice upon the world and individuals. But we must also look at how the hierarchical structure of the Church dampens its response within its own institutions.

The 1986 pastoral letter of the bishops of the United States, *Economic Justice for All*, calls for a "healthy economy" and "just wages," both terms subject to interpretation within and without Church circles.[23] These questions arise: How are women employees and volunteers treated by Church entities? Do they receive just wages? Do they find respect? Do they truly, as the saying goes "have a place at the table," even when their appointed positions seem to indicate they are to be listened to?

We must ask whether the institutional Church is capable of self-reflection in all these areas? Can criticism find a respectful hearing or does the specter of clericalism raise its dismissive head when internal issues—such as inequal pay and an inbred disrespect for women—form the kernel of institutional ignorance of the need to have a "preferential option for the poor," especially those for whom inadequate pay or an abuse of volunteer status are demeaning facts of their own inability to live freely and to be respected.

Moreover, when these same employees or volunteers speak, just as other poor and vulnerable persons in other settings, they find their voices stifled in the discussion. Too often, they are women, and more often than not, they are ignored.

## Rights and Responsibilities

That all persons have the right to be respected is woven throughout Catholic Social Teaching. All persons, it must be emphasized, include all women and girls, and all women and girls comprise the largest complement of the poor, the abused, and the ignored in the world.

Again, Catholic Social Teaching has always defended the rights of individuals. *Rerum Novarum* affirms the right to own property and *Dignitatis Humanae* defends the right to religious freedom. The list of human rights is long: the right to establish a family, to self-determination, to independence, to private property, to participate in public life, to marriage, to work, and to rest, among others. In short, the claim to personal freedoms is supported in the development of Catholic Social Teaching, even though some are in collision with the determinations of governmental policies of some nation states.

In his apostolic exhortation *Familiaris Consortio* (November 22, 1981), Pope John Paul II wrote of the various ways the dignity of women is attacked:

> Unfortunately the Christian message about the dignity of women is contradicted by that persistent mentality which considers the human being not as a person but as a thing, as an object of trade, at the service of selfish interest and mere pleasure: the first victims of this mentality are women.
>
> This mentality produces very bitter fruits, such as contempt for men and for women, slavery, oppression of the weak, pornography, prostitution-especially in an organized form-and all those various forms of discrimination that exist in the fields of education, employment, wages, etc.[24]

John Paul II was no feminist, but he does seem to have gone as far as any pope might have been able to in 1981. He earlier defended the right of women to public involvement, specifically in the political sphere:

One cannot but observe that in the specific area of family life a widespread social and cultural tradition has considered women's role to be exclusively that of wife and mother, without adequate access to public functions which have generally been reserved for men.[25]

John Paul II's comments could be considered supportive of the rights of women to vote, and, by extension, to live independent lives.[26] Without question, the theme of motherhood and family, so prevalent in his other writings, is present in *Familiaris Consortio*, but his defense of women as fully human persons is important.

The acceptance of women as fully human persons is necessary in the recognition of their rights and dignity. No matter how many words flow from the Vatican, or from international governmental and nongovernmental bodies, women are still regarded as chattel in too many places in the world. In fact, chattel laws are still on the books in many countries, and in many more, it matters not whether women are legally considered property; they are treated as though they are. According to the United Nations, in 19 of 189 member states laws explicitly require women to obey their husbands, and in 17 states women cannot travel outside the home unaccompanied. In 37 countries, women cannot independently apply for a passport.[27]

We cannot overlook the fact that, in his Letter to the Ephesians, Paul argues for the subservience of women: "Wives, be subject to your husbands as you are to the Lord" (Eph 5:22), which even Saint John Chrysostom used as a point of reference.[28]

Meanwhile, as recently as March 2022, the United Nations Commission on the Status of Women again pointed out that women are disproportionately bereft of effective voices in the halls of power:

Achieving gender equality and the empowerment of all women and girls and women's full, equal effective and meaningful participation and decision-making in the context of climate change, environmental degradation and disaster risk reduction is essential for achieving sustainable development, promoting peaceful, just and inclusive societies, enhancing inclusive and sustainable economic growth and productivity, ending poverty in all its forms and dimensions everywhere and ensuring the well-being of all.[29]

The Church remains at odds with certain statements, particularly those regarding reproductive issues, of the Committee on the Status of Women, which in its latest document affirms the 1995 Beijing Declaration and Platform for Action of the Fourth World Conference on Women (September 4–15, 1995) and was adopted by 189 countries.[30] Yet the Church cannot deny that women make up the poorest, most mistreated sector of society. Does the mistreatment of women extend to the Church?

The question remains: How is "women's full, equal effective and meaningful participation and decision-making" evidenced inside Church organizations and structures, particularly those that are controlled by clerics? There is a long and deep history of women decision-makers inside women-created and women-run organizations—schools, hospitals, social service agencies—but precious few women are at or even near the seats of power in chanceries or at the Vatican. Affirmations of the abilities of women notwithstanding, too often, women in positions of seeming authority only appear to have input in decision-making.

Clearly, there are clerics who can work with women as adult equals, but there are many who are not so able.[31] While Catholic Social Teaching affirms that all persons have the right to be respected, and all persons have the right and the responsibility to be involved, there are too many places where—whether in Church or in public or corporate life—such is not the case.

The papal encyclicals generally considered as forming the bedrock of Catholic Social Teaching are listed in Appendix I. Unfortunately, in their creation, women are barely mentioned, if at all. Where women are mentioned, there are increasingly hopeful comments about their dignity and rights, but there is a constant default to the primary role of woman as that of wife and mother, which, if poorly received, can be interpreted as an insistence by the Church that women can only

*[handwritten margin note: lot to do with abstinence]*

serve to propagate and keep house. Without denying the importance of these vocational options, it is necessary to recognize that longer life spans include more time for personal development, education, and service for those who choose marriage, as well as to recognize the various vocations outside marriage for the women who are unmarried for whatever reason, whether by choice or not.[32]

# 2

# Synodality

Until recently, Christianity's deep history of synodality had waned to be little more than a memory. While the Second Vatican Council attempted to revive the practice, the Church enjoyed uneven progress until Francis's pontificate. His initiation of a two-year, now three-year "Synod on Synodality" in October 2021 created confusion, complaint, and downright obfuscation in many quarters. Some national and regional episcopal conferences accepted the call and put great resources toward the project. Others did not. Similarly, individual dioceses had differing reactions to the entire process.

How does this affect women in the Church? Simply, a general complaint levied across the board by women of every age and relationship with the Church is that women are not listened to or, if they are listened to, they are not "heard." That is, whether speaking to pastors or bishops or, indeed, to any priest, they are met with condescending nods, and their recommendations, requests, and even complaints are ignored. Of course, this is a principal symptom of the clericalism infecting the entire Church.

Yet the new synodal processes initiated by Francis have met with responses that are designed to be inclusive of women and other marginalized groups and individuals. These responses come mostly from lay-controlled nonprofit organizations and women's religious institutes and orders that have worked to promote full and complete engagement with the synodal process as it has been defined (or redefined) for the 2021–2024 Synod on Synodality. As the Synod website states and promises,

> Pope Francis is calling on all baptized Catholics and all people of good will to enter into conversation and discernment with him, the bishops and one another about the future of the church.
>
> The Pope is making a special invitation to everyone on the peripheries and edges of the church. Your input and participation are central to this once in a generation opportunity to shape the future vision of a church that you can believe in, a church that learns as well as teaches. We are the teachers. We are the protagonists.[1]

In the past, women have not been in the forefront of synodal discussions, nor was there significant movement regarding their inclusion at various levels. This fact remains despite the many topics that touch on the experiences of women—both inside the Church and in society in general—within recent synodal discussion, especially regarding Catholic social justice principles as they are, or are not, applied to women.

## A BRIEF HISTORY OF SYNODS

An important document on synodality, published in 2018 by the International Theological Commission (ITC) of the Congregation for the Doctrine of the Faith (CDF), outlines the history and spirit of synods and synodality. There have been synods since the dawn of Christianity, and the Greek term σύνοδος (*sýnodos*), in the words of the ITC, "expresses how the disciples of Jesus were called together as an assembly and in some cases it is a synonym for the ecclesial community."[2] The word literally means "walking together," and, as explained by Saint

John Chrysostom, invokes the concept of the Church being the entire assembly of members, giving thanks and glory to God.

In general, the term has been applied unevenly to Church assemblies of various levels. While the Latin translation of the Greek for synod is "council," until Vatican II the terms were used interchangeably. The 1983 Code of Canon Law makes several distinctions between and among councils (plenary, provincial, ecumenical) and synods (of bishops or dioceses).

The important point, no matter the terminology, is that the meetings required consensus. Cyprian of Carthage wrote that nothing should be done without the consensus of the bishop, his council (priests and deacons), and the people.[3] The Apostolic Canons, for example, called for the local bishop not to act except with the agreement of his senior bishop, who in turn was not to act without the "consensus of all."[4]

The process and its definitions changed more in application than in meaning over the centuries, until Vatican Council I (1869–1870) endorsed papal primacy and stated that the doctrine of papal infallibility did not render the consensus of the Church superfluous. Rather, Vatican I affirmed papal consultation with the bishops and with the people of God.

However, processes of synodal discussion involving the entire people of God were not so evident, despite prescient writers who argued for its restoration in the modern era. The seeds of restoration had been sewn by Leo XIII, when he convoked the plenary council of the Latin American bishops in 1899, presenting what the International Theological Commission termed "a growing awareness" that "the Church is not identical with her pastors; that the whole Church, by the action of the Holy Spirit, is the subject or 'organ' of Tradition; and that lay people have an active role in the transmission of the apostolic faith."[5]

The "ongoing collaboration of the episcopate" was a thought for the future when presented in a speech by Milan's archbishop, Cardinal Giovanni Montini, on the death of Pope John XXIII.[6] Later, as Paul VI, Montini spoke several times of the necessary collaborative nature of the bishops of the world with the pope, including at the opening of the second session of Vatican II (September 29, 1963) and at its closing (December

4, 1963). But that was collaboration with bishops, not with the people of God, and certainly not with the women of the Church.

The *aggiornamento* of Vatican II—formally the Second Ecumenical Vatican Council—reintroduced and expanded synodality as a constitutive element of church, through *Lumen Gentium*, the Dogmatic Constitution of the Church (November 21, 1964). While the word *synodality* is not present in the document, *Lumen Gentium* does present what the International Theological Commission termed the "theological presuppositions of a suitable re-launch of synodality":

> The mystical and sacramental conception of the Church;
> her nature as People of God on pilgrimage through history
> towards the heavenly homeland, in which all her members
> are by virtue of baptism honoured with the same dignity
> as children of God and appointed to the same mission; the
> doctrine of sacramentality of the episcopate and collegiality in hierarchical communion with the Bishop of Rome.[7]

Paul VI spoke again of synodality as he opened the Council's final session on September 14, 1965. During this final speech, he announced the institution of a Synod of Bishops to consult with the pope "when for the well-being of the Church it might seem to him opportune."[8]

Paul VI's later decrees, *Christus Dominus* (October 28, 1965), together with its earlier companion decree for the Eastern Catholic Churches, *Orientalium Eccelsiarum* (November 21, 1964), present the synodal plan for the Catholic Churches. These, along with his apostolic letter *Apostolica Sollicitudo* (September 15, 1965), explain Paul VI's establishment of the Synod of Bishops.

Without doubt, the process, up to this time, was to be controlled by and include only men. As Paul VI wrote, "The Synod of Bishops is to have a permanent General Secretary, with a suitable number of assistants assigned to him. In addition, any Session of the Synod of Bishops is to have a Special Secretary of its own who remains in office until the end of the Session."[9] The listing of who would attend meetings of the synod of bishops sets the numbers of bishops to represent their individual episcopal conferences in addition to the presidents of these conferences, the cardinals heading departments of the Roman Curia, and three religious representing "clerical religious institutes."[10] Members of the laity are not mentioned.

Up until the papacy of Francis, there were thirteen ordinary, two extraordinary, and ten special synods of bishops (see Appendix II). During these synods, there was little note of Catholic Social Teaching, and less of the impact of local and world events on women. The focus of the ordinary synods was mainly internal.

During the papacy of Paul VI, ordinary synods addressed the revision of canon law and the creation of the International Theological Commission (1967), priesthood (1971), and evangelization (1974), while his extraordinary synod concerned episcopal conferences (1968).

The ordinary synods convened by John Paul II were on catechesis (1977), the Christian family (1980), penance (1983), the laity (1987), priestly formation (1990), and religious life (1995). John Paul II's extraordinary synod celebrated the thirtieth anniversary of the conclusion of Vatican II (1995), and his special synods addressed the Church in Holland (1980), Europe (1991), Africa (1995), Lebanon (1997), America (1997), Asia (1999), Oceania (1998), and Europe (1999).

Benedict XVI convened ordinary assemblies of the synod of bishops on the Eucharist (2005), the Word of God (2008), and the New Evangelization (2012). He convened two special assemblies of the synod of bishops on Africa (2009) and the Middle East (2010).

Given the range and scope of the special synods, it is not surprising that Francis, the first pope from South America, would convoke a synod on the Amazon in 2019. But prior to that, he held the Synod on the Family.

# SYNOD ON THE FAMILY (2014–2015)

Pope Francis was elected on March 13, 2013, and installed six days later, on the following March 19. By October 8 that year, he announced an Extraordinary General Assembly of the Synod of Bishops on the family and evangelization. It soon became apparent that the Extraordinary General Assembly would be followed one year later by the Fourteenth Ordinary General Assembly of the Synod of Bishops, which then took place in Rome October 4–25, 2015. After these two events, Francis issued his apostolic exhortation, *Amoris Laetitia*, "The Joy of Love."

Note that Francis called an Extraordinary General Assembly of the Synod of Bishops—only the third in addition to those in 1969 (on episcopal conferences' cooperation with the Holy See) and 1985 (on the twentieth anniversary of Vatican II)—very soon after his election. The stated theme of this Third Extraordinary General Assembly was "the pastoral challenges of the family in the context of evangelization."

Clearly, this new pope from Argentina had his finger on the pulse of the entire Church, not just that of the clerical caste. There was cautious hope that he would pay attention to the needs of the people of God. That hope would not be misplaced.

The Extraordinary Synod took place in the Vatican October 5–19, 2014. The usual people attended: presidents of episcopal conferences, members of the synod of bishops, with representatives from the Eastern Catholic Churches and secular and religious lay auditors.

As with previous synods, a preparatory document, then a working document (*Instrumentum laboris*), laid out the platform for discussion and commentary. The preparatory document gave the purpose of both assemblies, stating their endeavor "to define the '*status quaestionis*' [current situation] and to collect the bishops' experiences and proposals in proclaiming and living the Gospel of the Family in a credible manner."[11]

The preparatory document presented a basic catechesis and asked the bishops of the world to provide comment on nine questions about pastoral care for marriages and families, including (1) evidence of the dissemination of Church teaching; (2) marriage and natural law; (3) pastoral care of the family, in general; (4) and those in "certain difficult marital situations"; (5) same-sex unions; (6) education of children in "irregular marriages"; (7) openness to parenthood; (8) relationship between families and their individual members; and (9) other challenges the bishops wish to present.[12]

The second document, the *Instrumentum laboris* or working document, stated that the synod would "thoroughly examine and analyze the information, testimonies and recommendations received from the particular Churches in order to respond to the new challenges of the family."[13]

Depending on the reader, the preparatory document's topics can be received as pastoral considerations or outright challenges to their perceptions of Catholic teaching. The insurmountable fence seemingly erected around Church membership by some Catholic teachings, for example, those barring anyone other than a man and a woman, who intend to have children in a Church-ratified marriage, from receiving Holy Communion, has long been a sore point for persons not in that category. To even speak about topics beyond the given norm was surprising enough, but the eventual tone of the discussion helped bring Francis to the world stage as more of a pastor and less of a law enforcer.

As pope, Francis had already shocked the world with a response to a question about the oft-mentioned "gay lobby" in the Vatican, as he spoke with reporters on the plane returning him from his first pastoral visit, which brought him to Brazil for Catholic World Youth Day and other events in and about Rio de Janeiro, including to Aparecida do Norte, the site of the 2007 Fifth Episcopal Conference of Latin America, for which then-Cardinal Jorge Bergoglio chaired the document drafting committee.

During his 2013 return flight from Brazil, Francis spoke a sentence that circled the globe: "If a person is gay and seeks God and has good will, who am I to judge?"[14] The pope thereby affirmed the frequently misunderstood fact that, while homosexual acts were considered sinful, homosexual orientation was not, something he reaffirmed in his 2016 interview with Italian journalist Andrea Tornelli,[15] who since December 2018 has been editorial director of the Vatican's Dicastery for Communication.

On that same 2013 plane trip, Francis affirmed the Catholic Church's position against ordaining women as priests, while suggesting that women could and should have a greater role in the Church. He has both reaffirmed the ban and restated the need for a greater role for women in the Church several times.[16]

Some fourteen months after his trip to Brazil, the first of the two synods took place. Francis's written response to both was his post-synodal apostolic exhortation *Amoris Laetitia*, which begins, "The Joy of Love experienced by families is also the joy of the Church." At the outset of the document, the pope signals a subsidiarity clearly available to the Church, but relatively unknown in previous pontificates. He writes,

> Since "time is greater than space," I would make it clear that not all discussions of doctrinal, moral, or pastoral issues need to be settled by interventions of the magisterium. Unity of teaching and practice is certainly necessary in the Church, but this does not preclude various ways of interpreting some aspects of that teaching or drawing certain consequences from it.[17]

The section above, and the trajectory of the entire document, leads toward individual pastoral consideration and determinations based on individual pastoral situations.

That is, there is no one uniform application of the law that suits every situation. *Amoris Laetitia* does not overturn law, it provides guidelines on the application of the law in the light of the charity and mercy of the gospel. Hence, the eruptions in conservative circles about the now-infamous footnote 351, which expands on the essential dilemma of determining sinfulness and access to sacraments—specifically to Holy Communion in various situations. The section and the footnote were generally interpreted as referring to individuals in what are termed "irregular" marriages, for whom annulment is not yet available or is not even an option. The paragraph in question states,

> Because of forms of conditioning and mitigating factors, it is possible that in an objective situation of sin—which may not be subjectively culpable, or fully such—a person can

be living in God's grace, can love and can also grow in the life of grace and charity, while receiving the Church's help to this end.[18]

The footnote for which reads,

> In certain cases, this can include the help of the sacraments. Hence, "I want to remind priests that the confessional must not be a torture chamber, but rather an encounter with the Lord's mercy" (Apostolic Exhortation *Evangelii Gaudium* [24 November 2013], 44: *AAS* 105 [2013], 1038). I would also point out that the Eucharist "is not a prize for the perfect, but a powerful medicine and nourishment for the weak." (ibid., 47: 1039)[19]

It is important to note that this paragraph and its explanatory footnote come at the end of a long and detailed discussion of and response to the matters discussed at the two synods on the family. For example, Francis notes the facts of women in refugee camps and women subjected to domestic verbal, physical, and sexual violence. These women are not free in any sense of the word. Some have been separated from their husbands, others choose to leave them and their abuse behind. How can their situations be rectified if they choose to remarry, often for the sake of their children? In this consideration, it is important to note that the word *dignity* appears thirty-one times in *Amoris Laetitia,* often in defense of the dignity of women.

That the public media so easily collapsed the entire document into one phrase—"Communion for the divorced and remarried"—obviates the intent of the pastoral recommendation that persons be ministered to individually.

What slipped away, from both the apostolic exhortation and its resulting discussion, is that at least one synodal intervention was overlooked. In fact, the French-English synod communications briefer ignored the comment by Canadian Archbishop Paul-André Durocher of Gatineau, who seemed to connect the abuse of women by their husbands with the Church's unwillingness to restore the tradition of ordaining women as deacons.[20] That women deserved ministry by women was a given. Durocher stated quite clearly, "There has been no dogmatic statement saying that women cannot be ordained deacons."[21]

Francis did not react to Durocher's intervention. Perhaps his comments about marriage in *Amoris Laetitia* had caused enough of a stir.

# SYNODALITY TODAY (*EPISCOPALIS COMMUNIO*)

Francis had several other items in his to-do list, but before announcing another synod, he changed the way the Church held synods. On September 15, 2018, just before the opening of the Fifteenth Ordinary General Assembly of the Synod of Bishops, commonly referred to as the Synod on Young People, Pope Francis promulgated his apostolic constitution, *Episcopalis Communio*, on the Synod of Bishops. In it, he changed the norms for calling and conducting synods.[22]

By now, the Church was understanding that Francis's concept of synodality was far larger than the convening of a relatively small gathering of the world's bishops that had become *de rigueur* for synods.[23] True, *Episcopalis Communio* recalls that the Synod of Bishops was created as an "instrument of shared knowledge among the Bishops," who would meet with "common prayer, [and] honest exchange, [for a] deepening of Christian doctrine, reform of ecclesiastical structures and promotion of pastoral activity throughout the world."[24] These arrangements, however, assumed, but did not guarantee, inclusion of the questions and considerations of the whole people of God, including women.

In theory, the diocesan bishop would know the needs and hopes of the people he served. Yet in his apostolic constitution, Francis implies that what may be a given is not always so.

Francis wrote,

> The Bishop is both teacher and disciple. He is a teacher when, endowed with the special assistance of the Holy Spirit, he proclaims to the faithful the word of truth in the name of Christ, head and shepherd. But he is a disciple when, knowing that the Spirit has been bestowed upon every baptized person, he listens to the voice of Christ speaking through the entire People of God, making it "infallible *in credendo*."[25]

Saying that the "voice of Christ" is speaking through the "entire People of God" is not the locution of a lawgiver. The concept that the entire Church, not only the bishops (and the assembled bishops in synod at that) could know and speak the wishes of Christ is, again, as theologically sound as it is astonishing.

In *Episcopalis Communio*, the bishop is called to be a leader who listens to the people, and a disciple who believes they, too, can be the "voice of Christ." In calling for the bishop to listen "to the voice of Christ speaking through the entire people of God, making it "infallible *in credendo*," or, "in believing," Francis breaks open the barriers to a synodal discussion that was too apt to become both insular and circular.

In fact, Francis was reclaiming something determined at Vatican II, thereby attempting to rescue synods from being echo chambers for episcopal interests. The term *in credendo* refers to the statement in *Lumen Gentium*: "The entire body of the faithful, anointed as they are by the Holy One, cannot err in matters of belief."[26]

The question is what constitutes "belief."

Of course, the Synod of Bishops would do well if the bishops in attendance were attuned to their flocks. No one can disagree with that. But is that a given? What about "the entire body of the faithful"? What about the people on the margins—the periphery—that Francis has called the center of the Church?

So, why not have other members of the Church at the synod? Could the people of God be better served if their voices were heard at the assemblies of the synods of bishops? Could the whole Church be better served, could the resulting final document of the synod genuinely be "infallible *in credendo*" if the laity had input? Would the result be more in keeping with the developing doctrine of the Church if everyone in attendance, not just the bishops, had a vote?

# SYNOD ON YOUNG PEOPLE, THE FAITH, AND VOCATIONAL DISCERNMENT (2018)

In retrospect, the web page of this synod is as striking as it is prescient. Francis is pictured walking with eight young people, three women and five men, including two in Roman collars. On closer inspection of the image, however, it is obvious that the pope is walking hand in hand with three young women and three young men the front row. The two men in Roman collars standing behind them appear to have been photoshopped into the picture.

As the synod was being prepared, it became obvious that Francis was interested in listening to more than only bishops. The synod office prepared and presented an online questionnaire made available between mid-June and December 2017, which garnered more than one hundred thousand completed responses from persons between the ages of sixteen and twenty-nine around the world. The collection and coding of the responses, many qualitative, resulted in a 160-page sociological study, *The World of New Generations according to the Online Questionnaire*.[27]

In addition, an International Seminar on young people gathered three hundred young persons in Rome in September 2017 and an additional fifteen thousand through social media. Both efforts contributed to the synod's *Instrumentum laboris*.

Early on, the synod's Final Document recognizes that the difference between men and women "can give rise to forms of domination, exclusion and discrimination from which every society, including the Church, needs to be freed."[28] Later, echoing the need for the Church itself to be freed of stereotypical exclusion of women, the document notes,

> The young also clamour for greater recognition and greater valuing of women in society and in the Church. Many women play an essential part in Christian communities, but often it is hard to involve them in decision-making processes, even when these do not require specific ministerial responsibilities. The absence of the feminine voice and perspective impoverishes debate and the Church's journey, depriving discernment of a precious contribution. The Synod recommends that everyone be made more aware of the urgency of an inevitable change, not least on the basis of anthropological and theological reflection on the reciprocity between men and women.[29]

The need for anthropological and theological reflection upon the place of women in the Church is amplified and supported much later in the document, which recognizes that, while most of Jesus's disciples lived ordinary day-to-day lives, some women "shared the itinerant and prophetic existence of the Master (cf. Luke 8:1–3)."[30] The document also notes that "the vocation to the permanent diaconate calls for greater attention, because the full potential of this resource has yet to be tapped."[31] But what constitutes "anthropological and theological reflection"? Does the Church really need to agree as a body that women are made in the image and likeness of God? Is the Church so bereft of Christian theology that it subscribes to a dual nature anthropology—that men and women are of distinct natures, thereby not equal, thereby not able to image Christ?[32] Are the structures of the Church so encrusted by the past that they cannot accommodate women?

Francis's response to the Final Document, his post-synodal apostolic exhortation, *Christus Vivit*, is addressed to young people and to the entire people of God. Such is a far cry from the formalities of the past when popes addressed only bishops and clergy. In asking aloud how the Church might be able to respond to the dreams presented by young people, Francis wrote that the truth of the gospel does not exclude the possibility that the Church has not yet fully understood it:

> For example, a Church that is overly fearful and tied to its structures can be invariably critical of efforts to defend the rights of women, and constantly point out the risks and the potential errors of those demands. Instead, a living Church can react by being attentive to the legitimate claims of those women who seek greater justice and equality. A living Church can look back on history and acknowledge a fair share of male authoritarianism, domination, various forms of enslavement, abuse and sexist violence.[33]

Without digressing to discuss the horrific abuses of women individually by clerics and their abuse as a group by the clerical caste, it is important to note here that Francis implies that Church structures in and of themselves may present the greatest threat to "the rights of women," as he presents them, and that the Church is required by its very nature to at least be attentive to "the claims of those women who seek greater justice and equality."

Francis's words should be a clarion call to all Church members—both clerical and nonclerical—to do what they can to rid the Church of the scourge of clericalism—his term—that has roots in its very structures. Later, the pope acknowledges that "some young women feel that there is a lack of leading female role models within the Church,"[34] and, given the candor of the responses to the survey and the in-person meeting of the Youth Synod, he may be understating what the young women were talking about.

Overall, in his response to the synod, Francis's focus is on vocational discernment. Given that the role of conscience in discernment seems to have been a hotly debated topic during the synod—the sections about conscience received high percentages of negative

*[handwritten margin note: attracted to non clericalism identified as root issue]*

votes—and given his own admittedly Jesuit inclination toward serious discernment, one wonders how much about the issue the synod fathers understood.

The sections under "Conscience in Discernment" (106–9) are explicating what, in another time and another culture, the late Jesuit Father George Aschenbrenner called an "examination of consciousness."[35] Aschenbrenner clearly states that the practice of a daily examen as related to discernment is an examination of consciousness, not of conscience. The objective is to "find God in all things."

The reluctance of many synod fathers to affirm the sections on conscience and discernment is most probably reflective of rigid interpretation of certain tenets of moral theology relative to sexuality. Here it must be made clear that here or elsewhere, Pope Francis has not recommended situational ethics, but rather he teaches a pastoral approach to determinations of personal guilt and its consequences. As he has said, "Who am I to judge?"

In 2015, speaking to a crowd of young people in Paraguay at the end of his visit to three countries in South America, Francis urged them to "make a mess." He also encouraged them to help clean up the mess.[36] Whether the young people at the 2018 Youth Synod were sufficiently "messy" is unknown, since the members, and especially the relators of synodal discussion in the various language groups, were cardinals and bishops, many holding major Vatican appointments. Searches of the reports from the small group discussions rarely found the word *woman*. One English language group moderated by Cardinal Daniel DiNardo, archbishop of Galveston-Houston, with then-Los Angeles Auxiliary Bishop Robert E. Barron, directly requested the inclusion of the names of women in the final document, but only women of the Old Testament: Ruth, Deborah, Hannah, Abigail, and Tabitha.[37] As noted, the women who followed and supported Jesus were mentioned in the final document, citing Luke. The women mentioned in the Acts of the Apostles are not mentioned, nor is the deacon, Saint Phoebe (see Rom 16:1–2).

↳ seek to know more about biblical women

# AMAZON SYNOD (2019)

On October 15, 2017, while preparations for the synod on youth were still underway, Francis announced a special assembly of the synod of bishops from October 6 to 27, 2019. The new synod would be the Synod of Bishops for the Pan-Amazon Region.

The intent of this special assembly was "to identify new paths for the evangelization of God's people in that region." Included were the eight countries bordering the Amazon River in South America: Brazil, Bolivia, Colombia, Ecuador, Guiana, Peru, Suriname, Venezuela, and the territory of French Guiana. The entire area includes more than one third of the world's primary forests.

Francis, whose ministerial life took place mainly in South America, knew well the difficulties of the region. For example, by some estimates within the region's seven and a half million square miles live some thirty million persons in some four hundred tribes, many if not most in extreme poverty. The challenges to evangelization are clear. Some analyses count as many as three hundred languages belonging to multiple linguistic families.[38]

The grounds for the special assembly were prepared years earlier, with the creation of the Pan-Amazon Ecclesial Network (REPAM) in 2014, when the REPAM initiative began. It has three main characteristics: transnationality, "ecclesiality" or collaboration among Church groups and associations, and commitment to the defense of life.[39]

On May 24, 2015 (Pentecost), soon after REPAM was announced, Francis's encyclical on the environment, *Laudato Si'*, was promulgated. The announcement of the special assembly on the Amazon underscored his interest and intent on both the evangelization of the people on the periphery and the respect for the Earth, centered now directly on the Amazon region.

The seven major goals of *Laudato Si'* are threaded throughout the special assembly's planning and work: care for the environment; response to the needs of the poor; analysis of ecological economics;

recommendations for simple lifestyles; ecological education; ecological spiritualty; and an emphasis on community involvement and action.

The Amazon Synod, as it came to be called, was chaired by Pope Francis's friend, Brazilian Cardinal Cláudio Hummes, OFM (1934–2022), former archbishop of São Paulo and former prefect of the Congregation for the Clergy. Reportedly, immediately following Francis's election, Hummes said, "Do not forget the poor." The advice from the Franciscan cardinal may have influenced Jesuit Jorge Mario Bergoglio's choice of the name Francis—*Il Poverello*, Saint Francis of Assisi. Since then, Pope Francis has demonstrated his intense interest in the poor and marginalized people.

As the world waited, watching the unfolding of the Amazon Synod, it became apparent that two possibilities were uppermost in the minds of the media: married priests and women deacons. Neither the environment, nor the peoples of the Amazon, nor the application of the gospel to the region's troubles took up the greatest amount of public media space. The place of women in the Church and the possibility of ordaining married male deacons as priests seemed more interesting, especially as reporters and others gleaned what information they could about what was happening in the nonpublic discussions within the synod hall. Vatican press conferences often served to feed that interest, as various synod participants voiced their opinions in response to questions on these central questions about sacramental ministry in the Amazon region.

The synod's Final Document, "The Amazon: New Paths for the Church and for an Integral Ecology," which the synod's 182 voting members (no women) and 100 nonvoting participants collaborated, did not wholly disappoint. It appears that not all who had a vote cast theirs, but the tallies included the approval of ordaining married men as priests (128 to 41; see no. 111); installing women as lectors and acolytes (160 to 11; see no. 102); and a decisive leaning toward, if not an actual request for, women as deacons (137 to 30; see no. 103):

> In the many consultations carried out in the Amazon, the fundamental role of religious and lay women in the Church

of the Amazon and its communities was recognized and emphasized, given the wealth of services they provide. In a large number of these consultations, the permanent diaconate for women was requested. This made it an important theme during the Synod. The *Study Commission on the Diaconate of Women* which Pope Francis created in 2016 has already arrived as a Commission at partial findings regarding the reality of the diaconate of women in the early centuries of the Church and its implications for today. We would 'therefore like to share our experiences and reflections with the Commission, and we await its results.[40]

That never happened. Pope Francis said that he would accept the challenge, even at one point saying that he would recall the original Commission, perhaps adding a few members.[41] Instead, on April 8, 2020, some five and a half months later, he created an entirely new Commission. That new Commission held at least two meetings, one in September 2021 and another in July 2022.[42]

It appears that nine of the Amazon Synod's twelve language groups supported restoration of women to the diaconate, despite some synod members incorrectly arguing that *Ordinatio Sacerdotalis* (1994), the apostolic letter of John Paul II forbidding women priests, applied as well to women deacons. Because the synod was a "special assembly," the individual interventions of its voting members were not made public. Therefore, comments made both on and off the record to various members of the media became the only source of information on women deacons and the somewhat related question of married priests.

In February 2020, Francis's *Querida Amazonia* appeared. In the fourteen thousand words of his *Beloved Amazon: Post-Synodal Exhortation to the People of God and All Persons of Good Will*, the pope defended the rights of the poor, asked for recognition of the Amazon's distinctive cultures, emphasized the fact that everything is connected, and stressed the need for inculturation in the Church.

The final section, on inculturation, spoke indirectly to the Pachamama controversy created by ultraconservative media as the synod was getting underway. Pachamama is an Incan "Earth Mother" fertility goddess known in the Andes. While Pachamama oversees planting and the harvest, the statue representing her at the presynod gatherings and at the Carmelite Church of Santa Maria in Traspontina in Rome, the REPAM headquarters, was obviously that of a pregnant woman. Hence, the stunt managed and performed by Austrian layman Alexander Tschugguel on October 21, in which he was videotaped stealing five statues from the church and throwing them into the nearby Tiber River, showed disrespect in several ways: disrespect for indigenous peoples and their ancestral heritages, disrespect for an image of a woman, and, most crushingly, disrespect for the depiction of pregnancy.[43]

Querida Amazonia, Francis's dream for the Amazon, did not meet the expectations of the many who had hoped for a loosening of the Church's restrictions on ordaining married men as priests, a proposal mentioned by Cardinal Hummes upon his nomination to the Congregation for the Clergy in 2006.[44] In many countries, from time to time, married men who are pastors or priests of other Christian denominations have been accepted to the Catholic Church and subsequently ordained as priests. A married priesthood, while not impossible, would be a departure from the general norm in the Latin Rite. The expectation, then, was that Francis would allow priestly ordinations of select married male deacons in the Amazon Region, if only on a case-by-case basis.

But Francis also emphasized that the synod's requests were best known by the synod members themselves, and that his response in Querida Amazonia should be read in tandem with the Final Document. As if to underscore his point, Querida Amazonia is signed at the Basilica of Saint John Lateran, Francis's *cathedra* as Bishop of Rome.

In the fourth chapter of Querida Amazonia, "An Ecclesial Dream," Francis presents implicit agreement with the requests, at least for married priests, possibly for women deacons and, in retrospect, absolutely for women to be installed as lectors and acolytes. With his apostolic letter *Spiritus Domini*, he modified Code of Canon Law to read, "Lay persons who possess the age and qualifications established by decree of the conference of bishops can be admitted on a stable basis through

*[handwritten marginal note: how is this not subjective?]*

the prescribed liturgical rite to the ministries of lector and acolyte" (Can. 203 §1).[45]

But he does much more in terms of his "dream" for the Church of the Amazon and perhaps the world.

# SYNOD ON SYNODALITY (2021–2024)

The Synod on Synodality, which the Synod Office initially termed "a two-year process of listening and dialogue," was scheduled to take place between October 2021 and October 2023, promising discernment on how the Church (*communion*)—the whole Church (*participation*)—can move along (*mission*) in the light of the Spirit. The key words are *communion, participation*, and *mission*.

That was then, and remains today, an exciting prospect in the life of the Church beyond the close of the Synod on Synodality. Even so, the synod's course was set by its methodology. On May 20, 2021, in a letter to Maltese Cardinal Mario Grech, the sixty-five-year-old secretary general of the Synod of Bishops, wrote to the bishops of the world asking for the names of the coordinators of their diocesan synods and announcing the opening of the synod in Rome on October 9 that year. He wrote,

> The Holy Father has invited me to remain 'open to everything that comes from the local churches' and directed that each ordinary would celebrate the opening of the Synod in his own diocese on October 17, 2021.

Grech also noted that before October 2021, his office hoped "to be able to contact every Episcopal Conference to dialogue directly in this preliminary phase."

Two problems were immediately apparent. First, the Synod Office request went directly to each diocesan bishop, asking for the name(s) of diocesan Synod coordinators. It was only sometime later that the episcopal conferences were involved. Second, while different things were occurring in different places around the world, each in its own way evidenced the difficulties of managing such a huge task.

And yet, the Church already knew about each obstacle. The efforts surrounding the youth synod proved these difficulties and displayed the results. The pope himself had said the process would be messy. Sociologists complained that it would be impossible to quantify qualitative responses. Some dioceses participated fully; others made half-hearted efforts; and some did not even let their parishioners know about the Synod, its purpose, or its recommended processes. In many places, the stated intentions of "listening and dialogue" were replaced by one-sided surveys, both on the diocesan and conference levels, and were not well advertised even within Catholic venues.

In the United States, merely half of the dioceses provided points of contact by November or December 2021. By May 2022, approximately 90 percent, 176 of 196 dioceses and eparchies, had named contacts.[46]

From around the world, nearly 98 percent of all bishops' conferences and synods of Eastern Catholic Churches worldwide appointed a person or an entire team to implement the synodal process and a large number of initiatives were set up to promote consultation and discernment to responded to the Rome Synod Office.[47]

Early on, the Synod Office reported the synodal process was welcomed in several African, Latin American, and Asian countries, and that in other places diocesan or national processes were being harmonized with the processes for the Synod on Synodality.[48]

In fact, it is virtually assured that whatever was presented by dioceses and possibly by other groups was processed by bishops' conferences and sent to Rome.

In some respects, to depend only on the dioceses or conferences to conduct all the synod discussions is to fall prey to a form of clericalism. The animating concept of the synod, itself, presented the opportunity for *all* people to be involved in the effort and for *all* people to dialogue and listen. That many feared the event would simply be an international complaint session may indeed have caused diocesan bishops to pay episcopal lip service to the entire process. In many places where there was an effort toward participation beyond the margins, individuals who felt marginalized, including and especially women, refused to participate. Their general lack of trust in ecclesial processes caused them to believe that the report (whether a one-page parish report, a ten-page diocesan report, or indeed, a ten-page conference report) was already written and it did not matter what they said or thought.

Even so, in the United States at least, many independent groups undertook the task of organizing their own synod sessions. Predictably, some of these sessions did present opportunities for complaints. Some worked; others did not. In many cases, widespread discussion identified the major problems the Church encountered in the stated purpose of "walking together": clericalism and the treatment of women by the Church. Often, the solution given to the latter was elimination of the former.

Insofar as the lack of trust of the hierarchy is concerned, the Synod's *vademecum* is explicit in its instructions about the reports:

> Each diocese can choose to prepare the synthesis either before or after the Diocesan Pre-synodal Meeting, as long as the fruits of that meeting are also incorporated into the diocesan synthesis. As much as possible, everyone should feel that his or her voice has been represented in the synthesis. As a model of transparency, the members of the drafting team as well as the process of synthesizing the feedback be made public once it has been drafted, as a touchstone for the journey of the diocese along the path of synodality. As much as possible, opportunities can be given to the People of God to review and respond to the content of the diocesan synthesis before it is officially sent to the episcopal conference.[49]

In the United States and elsewhere, the adopted process predicted the results. It is impossible to determine how and with what means bishops may have attempted to skew the results of whatever consultations they held, but the underlying distrust for the entire episcopacy, at least in the

United States, tainted the process from the beginning. Yet, even within those dioceses that participated, or appeared to participate, there outcome was not guaranteed.

That said, there are efforts of the people of God to participate in the synodal process, that is, where they find out about it at all. On January 11, 2022, the United States Conference of Catholic Bishops (USCCB) sent a letter asking Catholic-affiliated organizations and institutions to submit a report to its synod office by June 30, 2022. As a result, a significant number of independent groups held their own synodal listening sessions, reports from which the USCCB asked to be funneled through its "Region XVI," a nonterritorial virtual region established specifically to handle their reports.[50] Some of these independent groups had agendas they wished to promote; others simply wished to provide space for conversations among their members. They ranged from open and closed meetings by monasteries and religious institutes to multiple meetings organized by lay groups of every description.[51]

The USCCB synod office asked each group or organization to provide information about the demographics, the consultation context, the methodology, and the central themes and recommendations. Finally, the synod office asked directly, "How is the Holy Spirit calling your organization to participate?" It specified using a ten-page double-spaced Word document in twelve-point Times New Roman font with one-inch margins, and including up to ten items of supporting documentation, such as photos, videos, art, and so on.

No matter, open or closed, religious or secular, clerical or lay, so far (again, anecdotally) the overwhelming response in the United States and in many other countries centers on the way women, among others, are marginalized by clericalism. (Germany, Ireland, and Australia prepared their preliminary reports with these results.) Given the starkness of at least a few paragraphs in the Final Document of the Synod on Youth, the repetition of this basic problem is not surprising. The paragraph from the Final Document entitled "Women in a Synodal Church" states,

A Church that seeks to live a synodal style cannot fail to reflect on the condition and role of women within it, and consequently in society more generally. Young men and women ask this question forcefully. The fruits of such reflection need to be implemented through a courageous change of culture and through change in daily pastoral practice. A sphere of particular importance in this regard is the female presence in ecclesial bodies at all levels, including positions of responsibility, as well as female participation in ecclesial decision-making processes, respecting the role of the ordained minister. This is a duty of justice, which draws inspiration both from the way Jesus related to men and women of his day, and from the importance of the role of certain female figures in the Bible, in the history of salvation and in the life of the Church.[52]

*attraction*

Some people reacted negatively to the clause "respecting the role of the ordained minister," but that can be read as either exclusive or inclusive of women, depending on the reader's view of history, theology, and anthropology. No matter which, the rest of the paragraph presents what is becoming more obviously the question of the entire people of God, less perhaps those most infested with clericalism: What about women?

How can the Synod on Synodality affect, even change, the Church now and in the future? That depends on how its results are received and acted upon. If the Synod on Youth is a precursor to the Synod on Synodality, then one of the most contested paragraphs in the Final Document of the former provides a clue. Some 20 percent of the voting synod members voted against the following paragraph, entitled "The Synodal Form of the Church":

> The experience they shared has made the Synod participants aware of the importance of a synodal form of the Church for the proclamation and transmission of the faith. The participation of the young helped to "reawaken" synodality, which is a "constitutive element of the Church... as Saint John Chrysostom says, 'Church and Synod are synonymous'—inasmuch as the Church is nothing other

than the 'journeying together' of God's flock along the paths of history towards the encounter with Christ the Lord" (Francis, *Address for the Commemoration of the fiftieth anniversary of the institution of the Synod of Bishops*, 17 October 2015). Synodality characterizes both the life and the mission of the Church, which is the People of God formed of young and old, men and women of every culture and horizon, and the Body of Christ, in which we are members one of another, beginning with those who are pushed to the margins and trampled upon. In the course of the exchanges and the testimonies, the Synod brought out certain fundamental traits of a synodal style: this is the goal of the conversion to which we are called.[53]

Fully 20 percent of the voting synod members objected to this paragraph, to the notion that all the people of God participate in the life and mission of the Church. That fact, combined with the abject refusal of some diocesan bishops and some pastors to participate wholeheartedly in current synod processes presents a stark reality: clericalism is deeply embedded in the structure of the Church and the division between clerics and laity may be unable to be bridged, let alone erased.

Of course, we cannot forget that all women are laypersons, and that laypersons are "outsiders." And so, can we not acknowledge the genuine fear that the "outsiders," remain unheard, unincorporated, and unable to gain genuine respect?

# 3

# Women and the Church

Despite the hoped-for implementation of changes suggested by Vatican II, women are assumed to have been legislated out of governance and jurisdiction by Church law that forbids their ordination to any grade of order. Specifically, canon 129 of the Code of Canon Law indicates that clerics are qualified by virtue of their ordination for governance and jurisdiction. Concurrently, laypersons may cooperate in these powers, although they may not possess them.[1]

While *Praedicate Evangelium,* the new apostolic constitution, can promise women positions within the Roman Curia, some have argued that certain offices require ordination, specifically, those in the Dicastery for Clergy and the Dicastery for Bishops. Pope Francis did name three women—two women religious and one consecrated virgin—as members of the Dicastery for Bishops, but the episcopal nominations they will be vetting come from apostolic nuncios, who in turn, receive nominations from among diocesan bishops. That is, the dossiers of the individuals the women will review, along with the other members of the dicastery, are prepared and presented by clerics, their names having been forwarded by apostolic nuncios.[2]

This raises two points: first, the Curia is the pope's staff, and so any authority is essentially delegated; second, Francis's rescript to canon 588 §2 published on February 11, 2022, allows for nonclerical local or major superiors in mixed clerical-lay institutes.[3]

The new apostolic constitution solidifies the fact that the Curia is the pope's staff. Some, if not all, curial staffers may also be involved in sacramental ministry, but the Curia's revamping implies that any layperson may obtain an office not otherwise restricted to the ordained (e.g., a bishop of a diocese). It affirms that any qualified lay Catholic may take up essentially managerial (as opposed to sacramentally ministerial) positions.

The rescript allowing nonclerical, that is, lay superiors in mixed clerical and lay institutes and orders recognizes their canonical authority and thereby their ability to choose superiors from among their members for internal positions as they see fit, again distinguishing between oversight and coordination functions and those that are specifically sacramental ministries.[4]

While the confirmation of laymen and -women into managerial staff positions and positions of authority in what have historically been lay-led institutes and orders is important, remaining lay-clerical tension blocks genuine synodality. It is important, however, to note that *Praedicate Evangelium* speaks of "the synod," not "the synod of bishops," so there could be more within it than one might think. Historically, women have been ordained as deacons. Consecrated abbesses, many of whom also were ordained deacons, have held absolute authority and jurisdiction over lands and persons. Should the history of women in authority be recovered or should new ways of incorporating women into "church" be attempted, or both?

# *PRAEDICATE EVANGELIUM*

Pope Francis's apostolic constitution *Praedicate Evangelium* reorganizes the papal Curia. Released on March 19, 2022, solely in Italian and put into effect the following June 5 (the Feast of Pentecost), the document is forthright in defining the role of "the Roman Curia and its service to the Church and to the World."[5] Furthermore, its title underscores the task of the Curia, the pope, and the entire Church: "Preach the Gospel."

The Curia has been reorganized several times since its formation.[6] This most recent reorganization is the result of nine years of discussion and consultation among Francis and the members of his council of cardinals, which originally comprised cardinals from each continent. The C-9, as it came to be called, did not initially include Cardinal Pietro Parolin, secretary of state, who had been attending meetings and was added as a member in 2014. When *Praedicate Evangelium* appeared, in addition to Parolin, the members were Óscar Andrés Rodríguez Maradiaga, SDB, archbishop of Tegucigalpa, Honduras (coordinator); Giuseppe Bertello, president of the Pontifical Commission for the Vatican City State; Oswald Gracias, archbishop of Bombay, India; Reinhard Marx, archbishop of Munich and Freising, Germany; Seán Patrick O'Malley, OFMCap, archbishop of Boston, USA, and president of the Pontifical Commission for the Protection of Minors; and Fridolin Ambongo Besungu, OFMCap, archbishop of Kinshasa, Democratic Republic of Congo.[7]

What changed? One immediately notes two modifications: first, all the sections of the Curia previously called congregations, councils, or commissions are renamed dicasteries; second, as noted earlier, any member of the Church may serve in any capacity in each of the offices. With the renaming of all sections as dicasteries, there appears to be a change in the prior formal or informal ranking of offices.

The protection of minors, for example, is elevated to a permanent commission within the Dicastery for the Doctrine of the Faith. Given that so many persons, male and female, turned away and continue to turn away from the Church due to what appears to be an ongoing blight of sex abuse and concurrent episcopal cover-up around the world, it makes sense to insert the protection of minors more carefully into the curial structure.[8] On the one hand, the change may demonstrate that the Church now recognizes a problem, which researchers attach to poor seminary entrance selection, formation, and improper oversight. On the other hand, it could also discount whatever means had been taken to address the issues in years prior. That is, while the change may state that the Church is now paying attention, it concurrently (if only subtly) admits that the Church was not paying attention all along. Furthermore, to insert the commission into a dicastery may appear to be yet another cover-up, complicated by the fact that the commission's interim secretary is a priest inexperienced in child protection.

More positively, the emphasis on "the missionary conversion" of the Church and the Roman Curia, as noted in the very title of the apostolic constitution, presents the Curia as outward looking, an aspect critically necessary to the evangelical needs of the Church. During Francis's pontificate, *ad limina* visits by members of national episcopal conferences evolved. During recent prior pontificates, bishops visited various offices and were lectured to. Under Francis, bishops attending *ad limina* meetings learned about the work of the various offices and participated in open discussions about how these offices could and, more importantly, would assist them and address their needs.

The fact of the reorganization of the Curia is less striking than the assertion that any Catholic is eligible for any of its offices. Such is an affirmation of the trajectory of appointments during Francis's papacy, where both secular and religious women have been appointed or advanced to positions of increasing authority in various dicasteries. While both Pope John Paul II and Pope Benedict XVI appointed a few women to offices, Francis has stepped up the pace substantially.

For example, in 2014, Francis named a Brazilian sister, Luzia Premoli, SMC, as a member of the Congregation for the Evangelization of Peoples. In 2018, he appointed a Spanish sister, Carmen Ros Nortes, NSC, as the undersecretary of the Congregation for Institute of Consecrated Life and Societies of Apostolic Life. Then, in July 2019, seven women religious were appointed members of the Congregation for Institutes of Consecrated Life and Societies of Apostolic Life (CICLSAL).[9] Also in 2019, Brazilian journalist Cristiane Murray was named vice director of the Holy See Press Office, replacing Paloma García Ovejero, who had served in that capacity since 2016. In 2020, Francesca Di Giovanni was named to serve as the undersecretary for Multilateral Affairs in the

Section for Relations with States, perhaps the first woman to hold a managerial position within the Roman Curia.

The COVID-19 pandemic did not slow Francis down, as he continued to make important appointments of women to the Curia. In 2021, he named Sister Nathalie Becquart, XMCJ, one of two undersecretaries to the Synod of Bishops, she having been appointed consultor to that office two years prior.[10] In March 2021, Francis named Professor Nuria Calduch-Benages as the first woman secretary of the Pontifical Biblical Commission.[11] In November 2021, he appointed Franciscan Sister Raffaella Petrini as the first woman secretary general of the Pontifical Commission for Vatican City State, essentially as deputy to Archbishop Fernando Vergez Alzaga, LC. In 2022, she was named a member of the Dicastery for Bishops.[12]

Later in 2021, he appointed Professor Emilce Cuda from Argentina to head the Pontifical Commission for Latin America, and in February 2022, he promoted her to Secretary of the Commission, which now counts Cuda and a layman as coequal secretaries.[13]

These appointments, which are moving ahead with increasing speed, join others to lower-ranking positions within the various dicasteries, giving the Curia the opportunity to reset its predominantly clerical male culture. While striking in some respects, it is important to recall that women, especially women religious, have held influential positions in the Curia prior to Francis's pontificate. For example, from 1986 to 2001, American Marjorie Keenan, RSHM, was an official of the Pontifical Council for Justice and Peace, having been named a member of that council in 1977.[14]

Aside from personnel considerations, which are intuitively reflective of Francis's wish to have the entire people of God involved at multiple levels of the Church, the fact that *Praedicate Evangelium* (Preach the Gospel) replaces *Pastor Bonus* (The Good Shepherd) is a clear commentary on the direction the Curia may take in the months and years ahead, independent of the length of Francis's papacy. The apostolic constitution quite clearly prioritizes preaching the gospel and the missionary nature of the Church. The point of the constitution is not so much how to manage internal affairs as how to reflect and speak the

Church's "good news" throughout the world. That effort, combined with its emphasis on synodality, is complemented by the constitution's emphasis on the roles of various bishops' conferences.

As with any bureaucratic reorganization, with *Praedicate Evangelium* some offices have been combined, others downgraded, and as emphasized earlier, their upper echelons are no longer assumed to be the private preserves of clerics. Furthermore, the Curia is to be at the service of the world's bishops rather than an obstacle to their work: "The Roman Curia does not place itself between the Pope and the Bishops, but rather places itself at the service of both in the manner that is proper to the nature of each."[15] Similarly, episcopal conferences are not to place themselves between individual bishops and the pope, but rather to be in "full service" to them.[16]

The reorganization—some might call it streamlining—of the Curia replaced two sections of the Secretariate of State, nine congregations, twelve pontifical councils, and three tribunals in addition to combining or eliminating several other offices creating fewer units and thereby fewer fiefdoms. Implicit within the text of the constitution is the need to address the problem of turf wars, not unique to the Vatican's bureaucracy.

Francis had already combined some curial sections. By merging four pontifical councils—the Pontifical Council *Cor Unum*, and those for Justice and Peace, the Pastoral Care of Migrants and Itinerant People, and Health Pastoral Care—Francis created the Dicastery for Promoting Integral Human Development, still headed by a cardinal but with a woman religious as secretary, or second in command.

The combination of the Pontifical Council for Culture with the Congregation for Catholic Education resulted in the Dicastery for Culture and Education, which will have secretaries for each of its sections: culture and education.

In many respects, the combining of distinct curial bodies makes eminent sense, insofar as their related tasks can be better coordinated under a single prefect. Further, if the objective of redesigning the Curia is to ultimately reduce the numbers of employees in general and of resident clerics in particular, the constitution will likely accomplish the latter, if not the former.

With the reorganization, Francis reduced the number of dicasteries to sixteen. He also established a third section at the Secretariat of State, that to care for the Holy See's diplomatic personnel, joining those for the Relations with the States and the General Affairs of the Church. Furthermore, the constitution recovers an older title for the Secretariat of State—"the Papal Secretariat."

Following the Secretariat of State, at least in the listing, is the Dicastery for Evangelization, now listed ahead of what is now the Dicastery for the Doctrine of the Faith. That dicastery now has two sections and therefore two secretaries (one for doctrine; the other for discipline), as well as a third commission, that for the Protection of Minors (as noted earlier), in addition to the Pontifical Biblical Commission and the International Theological Commission, each of which is an external consultative body.

After these comes the Dicastery for the Service of Charity (formerly the Office of Papal Charities). While most people know this office as the place to obtain parchment papal blessings, in and of itself an innovation of Francis, who early on removed the selling of the parchments from the storefronts lining Via del Mascherino near the Porta Sant'Anna. Since then, all proceeds, or at least all profits from sales, are applied to works of charity.

One part of the Curia that has received significant media attention since Francis's election is the oversight of Vatican finances, and the new constitution describes in detail the ways in which financial matters are overseen, both in general and in each dicastery.

# ECCLESIOLOGY AND PARTICIPATION

The question of who does what plagues every bureaucracy, and the same is true for the organization of the Church. One can argue for or against bureaucracy, but for better or worse, the centralizing activity of the Vatican and the Roman Curia allows for a uniformity not completely recognizable in other denominations and religions.

There are clerics and nonclerics. Approximately 1 percent of Catholics are ordained clerics. The great majority of Catholics are "the laity." Comments like "pray, pay, and obey" indicate the relationship laypersons have had, and in many places still have, with the institutional Church. Few parishes enjoy full lay participation in decision-making, and fewer dioceses than even these parishes genuinely include lay voices. Transparency is an unrealized concept on many levels.

While the revised Code of Canon Law, which appeared in 1983, does affirm the rights, duties, and equality of all Christians, important caveats inserted into some canons negate that possibility. One section of *Lumen Gentium* lays out the important points:

> By divine institution Holy Church is ordered and governed with a wonderful diversity. "For just as in one body we have many members, yet all the members have not the same function, so we, the many, are one body in Christ, but severally members one of another." Therefore, the chosen People of God is one: "one Lord, one faith, one baptism"; sharing a common dignity as members from their regeneration in Christ, having the same filial grace and the same vocation to perfection; possessing in common one salvation, one hope and one undivided charity. There is, therefore, in Christ and in the Church no inequality on the basis of race or nationality, social condition or sex, because "there is neither Jew nor Greek: there is neither bond nor free: there is neither male nor female. For you are all 'one' in Christ Jesus."[17]

Here, the Council sees a Church "ordered and governed with a wonderful diversity," implying more than the reality then or now. As much as specifically managerial and staff positions are being opened to laypersons, the Church's ordering and governance are restricted to clerics. The new apostolic constitution does not change that scenario significantly.

For example, the rescript allowing mixed clerical and lay religious orders and institutes to elect lay superiors requires Vatican approval—the accession of the Dicastery for Institutes of Consecrated Life and Societies of Apostolic Life—on behalf of the pope. The process thereby essentially restricts affirmation of the election of a lay superior to the pope, and strictly clerical internal matters appear to require clerical oversight within the given institute or order. Even so, Francis's apostolic letter, *Ad Charisma Tuendum*, issued *motu proprio* in July 2022, legislates that the supreme moderator of the nonterritorial personal prelature, *Opus Dei*, will not be consecrated as a bishop, but rather may use the title "Apostolic Supernumerary Protonotary."[18]

However, germane to questions related to women in the Church, and specifically within religious institutes, is how women's orders historically led by consecrated abbesses who were often also ordained as deacons would be considered. But that does not seem to pose any problem relative to election of a lay superior, given that current restrictions only apply to priests.

Aside from the internal governance of orders or institutes, which are private organizations recognized by, but not comprising "the Church," the hope emanating from the above cited paragraph in *Lumen Gentium* seems misplaced in many respects. Initially, as mentioned above, there is no provision for the Church to be "ordered and governed" with any type of "diversity." The Church is ordered and governed by clerics.

Some revisions made in the 1980s to the Pio-Benedictine Code of Canon Law (promulgated by Pope Benedict XV with his apostolic constitution, *Providentissima Mater Eccelsia* [May 27, 1917]) include a nod to *Lumen Gentium* but seem to reverse its intent. For example, canon 208 of the revised 1983 Code reads,

> From their rebirth in Christ, there exists among all the Christian faithful a true equality regarding dignity and action by which they all cooperate in the building up of the Body of Christ according to each one's own condition and function.

The key word here, as in an earlier canon, is "cooperate."

# Governance and Jurisdiction

In the years during which the Code of 1917 was under revision, there were some recommendations that laypersons participate in governance and jurisdiction, at least in situations that did not require sacred orders. The above-mentioned rescript regarding the internal governance of men's religious orders and institutes presents an opportunity for such governance. In wholly lay orders and institutes, superiors have had and continue to have considerable authority.[19]

Governance in the Church is a different matter. As canon 129 was being drafted, in the spirit of *Lumen Gentium* 32 the initially proposed language of its second paragraph stated that laypersons could share (*partem habere*), as opposed to cooperate (*cooperari*) in the exercise of power (*potestas*). In 1981, at the first vote on the canon's wording during the *Plenaria* on the revised Code, most drafting committee members voted to include laity in governance and jurisdiction, that is, to codify as fact that laypersons (apparently both men and women) could share in the exercise of power.

There were two principal schools of thought—the so-called German school (more properly, the Munich school) and Roman schools—each in constant opposition to the other on the matter. Although the first vote was fifty-two in favor of *partem habere* with nine opposed, the text was eventually weakened so that the word "cooperate" replaced "share." That is, the possibility of laymen and laywomen exercising power was definitively ruled out.

The restrictive paragraph regarding the "power of governance… also called the power of jurisdiction" written by then-Archbishop Joseph Ratzinger and approved exactly as he composed it—excepting one comma—restricts laypersons from any Church-wide jurisdiction. Laypersons cannot share the power of governance. They can only cooperate with it. Canon 129 §2 states, "Lay members of the Christian faithful can cooperate in the exercise of this same power according to the norm of law."[20]

The change made to the 1983 Code had and still has deep ramifications. For example, when, in July 2022 some 254 members of the

Australian Plenary Council took up part 4 of the Plenary document, entitled "Witnessing to the Equal Dignity of Women and Men," it passed the so-called consultative vote but failed the "deliberative vote." The difference? The consultative vote was by lay members, deacons, and priests. The deliberative vote was by the bishops. In short, the bishops voted against women, especially and particularly against the sections regarding restoration of women to the ordained diaconate.[21]

Following the vote, and after a tea break, stunned Plenary Council members refused to take their seats. Some sixty persons, mostly women, but men and even a few bishops, stood at the back of the room in protest. An emergency meeting of the bishops ensued, and over lunch there was an agreement to amend the section and proceed with another vote. There were several subsections to part 4, but the most contentious issue seems to have been the question of women in the diaconate. As it happened, the rewritten part 4, including that on women deacons, passed both the consultative and deliberative votes two days after the widely reported failure of the first draft.

Part 4's Motion 4.5, as passed, reads,

> That, should the universal law of the Church be modified to authorize the diaconate for women, the Plenary Council recommends that the Australian Bishops examine how best to implement it in the context of the Church in Australia.

Some immediate problems with the motion as passed are apparent. First, the amended motion was amended. The clause "receive the possibility with openness," which had been inserted after "Australian Bishops," was removed, so that it did not read "the Australian Bishops receive the possibility with openness." That would be the possibility of women deacons.

Second, and more troubling, while a change in the universal law of the Church could imply a change to canon 1024, "A baptized male alone receives sacred ordination validly," what the Australian bishops finally agreed to could also imply a nonordained female diaconate parallel to but not equal to the present ordained diaconate.

Finally, the process by which the motion was approved left to the imagination the reasons why the bishops, in both the first and second instances, voted against women in the diaconate. The bishops' votes were secret, and no objector seems to have voiced his opinion or, surely, his vote. As it happened, thirty-seven of forty-three participating bishops approved the measure (32 positive votes were needed), one voted to approve with some modifications in addition to the deletion of the section noted above), and five still voted against the measure. Eighteen had voted against it in the original draft.[22]

In his Sunday homily following the vote, Jesuit priest Frank Brennan, the widely respected rector of Newman College in Melbourne, decried the lack of transparency on the part of the bishops, none of whom explained or even announced his vote. Was this an example of clericalism? As Brisbane Archbishop Mark Coleridge, president of the Australian Catholic Bishops Conference said, "The problem with explaining the vote, you run the risk of disclosing or disrupting the anonymity of the process. That's an essential part."[23]

So, actual power, in the Australian Plenary's deliberative vote as above, and canonically in Church governance and jurisdiction, is concentrated in clerics. Laypersons do not share it; they can only cooperate with it.

## Governance, Clerics, and Clericalism

The barriers to incorporating women into positions of Church governance and jurisdiction are both historical and canonical. Each supports the increasing infection of clericalism choking the Church. For women to be incorporated into positions of genuine authority, history must be recovered, and in some part overcome, and canon law must change, or at least be reinterpreted.

Title IX, the section on Ecclesiastical Offices in the revised Code of Canon Law of 1983 (canons 145–96), erects obvious barriers to the incorporation of women into positions of authority. In addition to the constrictions evident in canon 129, which eliminate the possibility of laypersons sharing governance and jurisdiction, the first paragraph of that same canon pronounces that ordination to "sacred orders" qualifies an individual for the "power of governance."[24] That is, apparently no other qualification is needed. While of course there are universal and local vetting procedures for appointing bishops and pastors, the statement embeds a peculiar point: ordination—and, it would appear, only ordination—qualifies an individual for the power of governance, with which, as previously noted, laypeople may only cooperate. Hence, one seed of clericalism.

Ecclesiastical offices are defined as "any function constituted in a stable manner by divine or ecclesiastical ordinance to be exercised for a spiritual purpose" (can. 145 §1). These offices distinguish within them powers of governance that are separated as legislative, executive, and judicial.

Briefly, executive power can be delegated and subdelegated. Legislative power below the pope cannot be delegated. Judicial power is not delegated but is ordinary with respect to a judge, even one who is appointed ad hoc. There can be only one lead person in a tribunal, led by either the judicial vicar or the adjutant judicial vicar as much as possible, and the judges sign the sentence.

In 2015, Pope Francis's change to the rules for marriage annulment proceedings allow for a single judge and eliminate the requirement for a mandatory review in what is termed a "second instance," that is, a second judicial review of a decision.[25] However, the single judge must be a cleric. Therefore, the possibility of lay involvement, specifically women's involvement, in the delicate matters surrounding the dissolution of a marriage is greatly reduced.[26] Anecdotally, most Church annulments are sought by women.

Without doubt, Francis intends to widen the Church's procedures and personnel to include greater representation of the people of God, especially as the numbers of Catholics reaches, even exceeds, 1.3 billion. His efforts may in large part be driven by the continued decline in the numbers of priests and religious worldwide, which, in turn, creates space for laymen and -women and, to be sure, deacons.

The scourge of clericalism might eradicate itself, as people leave the Church wherever it is most present. The new pastor or bishop who, in his initial months, seeks to overturn his predecessors' policies and remove long serving personnel, exemplifies a well-documented attitude. For him, clerical status is a badge of honor, his membership in an exclusive club, and evidence of his "right" to decide matters without consultation and consent. When the virus of clericalism spreads, whether solely in a parish or throughout a diocese, the people of God find themselves regarded as outsiders who, in the well-worn trope, are required to pray, pay, and obey to maintain membership.

The difference in the twenty-first century, at least in the United States and in other highly industrialized countries, is that laypersons, and especially women, are both better educated and in many cases better situated in the worlds of business, science, and service industries. Therefore, they do not receive imperiousness lightly, and are more likely to leave the given parish or diocese for another, or even for another Christian denomination. So-called John Paul II priests, who (often as late vocations) were ordained between 1978 and 2005, are now in their fifties and sixties and are increasingly moving into positions of parish or diocesan power and authority. These clerics now also supervise younger priests whose formation took place during the reign of Benedict XVI (2005–2013), and who too often display the attitude embedded in the concept attributed to Benedict: a "smaller, purer church."[27] The "smaller church" concept was espoused by other hierarchs, including then-Archbishop Charles Chaput of Philadelphia.[28]

With or without those exact words from the now-retired Bishop of Rome, who determined for himself what is inarguably the second-best clerical title in the world, *pope emeritus*, the attitude of take it or leave it—especially regarding questions of women's ministry, even questions of just treatment—is present in many rectories and chanceries.

Despite the supports for clericalism found within liturgical and canon law, and the disdain by many "clerical" clerics for the laity (and women, in particular), there is a growing understanding of precisely what Pope Francis meant by the term when he addressed the Synod Fathers in 2018 at the Synod on Young People: "Clericalism arises from an elitist and exclusivist vision of vocation, that interprets the ministry received as a power to be exercised rather than as a free and generous service to be given."[29]

Such is the definition, and such is the root of the problem. The ongoing presentation in seminaries of prospect of an ontological change at ordination, a change at the very nature of the being of the individual ordained, leads some priests to believe that their very existence has transubstantiated them into other Christs such that they are both distinct and above the ordinary Christian. In fact, the term *ontological change* comes from the work of Saint Thomas Aquinas, who explained that the eucharistic mystery as one in which the substance (the essence, or ontology) of the bread and wine changes during the Mass, while the accidents of these substances (their appearances) remain. It is defined Catholic teaching that the bread and wine become the Body and Blood of Christ while retaining their "accidental" properties or appearances.

An ontological change is also effected through the sacraments of Baptism and Confirmation; when it is understood incorrectly by an ordained individual that understanding may make him feel superior to laypersons. Yet, as Richard Gaillardetz has argued, the notion of ontological change can only be retained if the conferral of the identifying sacramental character of ordination is understood to identify the individual specifically as in relation to the Church as the people of God.[30] Gaillardetz further presents the notion of Greek Orthodox theologian John Zizioulas, who contends that all Church members are "ordained" by virtue of their baptism. Hence, all Church members are recipients of an ontological change configuring them to Christ.[31]

Therefore, the questions: First, if all persons are subject to ontological change by virtue of baptism, are all persons subject to ontological change through ordination? Second, how can females be baptized and confirmed and yet not be eligible for holy orders? And third, does clericalism itself create the basis for dismissive attitudes toward women in many sectors of the Church, which attitudes are mirrored in Christian and non-Christian societies around the world?

Pope Francis recognized clericalism as "a perversion" and "the root of many evils in the Church."[32] Can the Church recognize the same?

# WOMEN'S ROLES IN THE CHURCH

Relationships women have with the Church and clerics are increasingly fraught with an overlay of clericalism. Two general areas of interaction call into question the ways Catholic Social Teaching and synodality affect women. Women who, as religious or secular members of the Church are employed in various positions, and in some dioceses, as well as in Rome, are gaining paid employment in managerial positions. Some are employed in some dioceses in ministerial positions, as pastoral ministers, hospital chaplains, and so on. Some are employed by institutions owned and operated by men's or women's religious orders or institutes (schools, hospitals, social service centers). They and all other women are members of the laity. That is, all women are nonordained persons, whether seculars (married or single) or members of religious orders and institutes (sisters and nuns).

To understand and evaluate the ways women are treated in these situations as *employees*, one must look at how Catholic Social Teaching is applied. To understand and evaluate the ways women are treated as *lay members of the Church*, one can also look to Catholic Social Teaching, but only in light of synodal efforts worldwide. To be sure, some dioceses have ignored the call for synodality, and others have truncated the processes to keep questions regarding women in the Church from reaching their episcopal conferences, possibly hoping to avoid reporting the deep dissatisfaction of women, and specifically, the ways in which they are eliminated from influence and generally disrespected.

Can the hierarchical Church recover the attitude of Jesus toward women? Jesus is known to have had many women among his disciples. Given the culture and the eras during which the Gospels were written, it is extremely important to note the many women he counted among his disciples. As the Church grew and formalized both its managerial and ministerial positions, restricting ministry to sacramental ministry in many senses, history demonstrates that women were increasingly maltreated and pushed aside.

Horrific tales of bishops confiscating abbatial and monastic properties dot the annals of the Middle Ages, even though the authority of abbots and abbesses was repeatedly affirmed by councils. For example, as early as the Council of Arles (455), the rights and powers of the abbot of Lérin were affirmed over the authority of Bishop Theodoros of Frégus.[33] These types of disagreements continued across the centuries. Hildegard of Bingen (1098–1179) had her disputes with authority. From the time of its founding in the twelfth century until 1873, the abbess of the royal monastery of Santa María la Real de las Huelgas en Burgos held territorial ecclesiastical jurisdiction. She, along with the mitered abbess of San Benedetto, Conversano, Italy, and in fact all others lost these privileges with the promulgation of the Pius IX's Bull *Quae Diversa*.[34]

More recently, in the nineteenth century, Saint Mary MacKillop (Sister Saint Mary of the Cross, RSJ), Australian founder of the Sisters of Saint Joseph of the Sacred Heart, was briefly excommunicated by a bishop due to disagreements over their internal governance and control of their schools. In the case of Mary MacKillop and her sisters, Rome came to her aid; Pope Leo XIII granted approval of her congregation.[35]

Today, similar disagreements between diocesan bishops and religious continue, but their independent nature is increasingly recognized by the Vatican, as the rescript allowing lay superiors general evidences.

History is instructive, but because it is always incomplete, the hierarchical Church does not enjoy a proper understanding of the ways in which women have served the Church or the ways they have been ignored and misrepresented.

## History of Women Deacons

In the relatively recent past, the history of women in ordained ministry has become a topic fraught with claims and counterclaims, some with an ideological rather than an intellectual basis. The argument rests on the question of whether the women known as deacons or as deaconesses, whose lives and ministries are documented through literary and epigraphical sources, were or were not sacramentally ordained.[36]

The simple answer is yes. Yes, it is entirely possible some were not ordained; it is more likely that many others were sacramentally ordained. The latter proposition depends on whether ordination as deacon comprises a sacramental ordination.

Discussions on the nature of the ordinations of women in history appears to have begun in the seventeenth century, when French theologian John Morin (1591–1659), reviewing all the extant ceremonies, determined they met the criteria established by the Council of Trent for sacramental ordination.[37]

Some one hundred years later, Bollandist Jesuit Jean Pien (1678–1749) argued that despite clear evidence (particularly that of the laying on of hands and the *epiclesis*—the invocation of the Holy Spirit), the same ordinations were not sacramental.[38]

The controversy over whether women deacons were or were not ordained continues to this day, having been taken up again in the 1970s and 1980s by Roger Gryson and others in the affirmative, and Aimé-Georges Martimort in the negative.[39] Contemporary scholarship tends to agree with the affirmative position, while some writers now attempt to connect the priesthood and diaconate such that the possibility for women deacons is overruled due to statements about women priests.[40]

It is obvious from Scripture that women were among the disciples performing ministry. Furthermore, in Scripture, the only individual specifically named deacon is Saint Phoebe, whom Saint Paul entrusts with his Letter to the Romans (see Rom 16:1–2). Unfortunately, few hear about Saint Phoebe's charge in Latin churches and cathedrals because the lectionary ends its cycle of readings at the end of chapter 15 and then picks up the next day with Romans 16:3.

Similarly, while Saint Phoebe's feast had been celebrated on September 3, and is still celebrated on that date by Anglicans and in Orthodox Churches, in 1969, the revised Roman Catholic lectionary moved the obligatory memorial of Saint Gregory the Great from his date of death, March 12, to September 3, the date he became pope. The irony of Gregory overtaking Phoebe in Catholic liturgy is that, in his homily in September 592, he solidified Mary Magdalene (in his words) as a woman "full of vices."[41]

In the twentieth and twenty-first centuries, discussion about restoring women to the ordained diaconate grew following the discussion about the ministry at Vatican II. Council fathers voted to restore the diaconate as a permanent ordained ministry, but only for men. There was some discussion about women deacons, but that was essentially ignored.[42]

*Lumen Gentium* defined the diaconate as an ordained ministry and separate from the priesthood, and detailed diaconal duties as follows:

> At a lower level of the hierarchy are deacons, upon whom hands are imposed "not unto the priesthood, but unto a ministry of service." For strengthened by sacramental grace, in communion with the bishop and his group of priests they serve in the diaconate of the liturgy, of the word, and of charity to the people of God. It is the duty of the deacon, according as it shall have been assigned to him by competent authority, to administer baptism solemnly, to be custodian and dispenser of the Eucharist, to assist at and bless marriages in the name of the Church, to bring Viaticum to the dying, to read the Sacred Scripture to the faithful, to instruct and exhort the people, to preside over the worship and prayer of the faithful, to administer sacramentals, to officiate at funeral and burial services. Dedicated to duties of charity and of administration, let deacons be mindful of the admonition of Blessed Polycarp: "Be merciful, diligent, walking according to the truth of the Lord, who became the servant of all."[43]

The section above presents tasks and duties well-known and well-documented throughout history as tasks and duties taken up by women. There has been little academic dispute that women known as deacons (or deaconesses) ministered within their communities in the way prescribed in *Lumen Gentium,* often if not exclusively to women and children. The question arises: If the exclusion of women as deacons today is based on the assumption that the women deacons of history ministered only to women and children, then who ministers to women today?

The council document continues, however, to affirm the critical nature of diaconal ministry to all the people of God:

> Since these duties, so very necessary to the life of the Church, can be fulfilled only with difficulty in many regions in accordance with the discipline of the Latin Church as it exists today, the diaconate can in the future be restored as a proper and permanent rank of the hierarchy. It pertains to the competent territorial bodies of bishops, of one kind or another, with the approval of the Supreme Pontiff, to decide whether and where it is opportune for such deacons to be established for the care of souls.[44]

The import of this paragraph, which directly follows the definition of the deacon and the deacon's tasks and duties, cannot be overstated. Published in 1964, the document affirms that diaconal tasks and duties "can be fulfilled only with difficulty in many regions of the Latin Church as it exists today." That is, the Latin Church of 1964 had virtually no individuals ordained to the diaconate as a permanent vocation. The Catholic population was growing, yet projections for numbers of priests and religious began to show the sharp decline all too evident today.[45]

In fact, the Catholic world population has more than doubled between 1964 and today, and the number of ordained deacons has grown exponentially. By 1970, there were 309 deacons (none in the United States) and by 2018, there were 46,813 worldwide.

## Women in Lay Ministry

During the pontificate of Pope Francis, synods on the international, national, and local levels have brought questions about women in ministry to the fore. Clearly, women are involved in ministry in a variety of situations—as noted, in schools, hospitals, social service agencies, and parishes. In and through these settings, they serve as catechists, chaplains, and confidants.

There are two points of consideration. First, the need for ministry—to the poor, the outcast, and those on the peripheries of society. Second, the need to somehow accommodate the women now ministering as well as to plan for a future that incorporates women in ministry.

The Amazon Synod continued the energetic requests of prior synods—particularly that of the Synod on Young People—and brought the question of accepting women in all ministries to the discussion. As mentioned earlier, Francis's "ecclesial dream" for the future presented in *Querida Amazonia*, his response to the Amazon Synod's Final Document, implied that he acceded to the Amazon Synod's request for women to be installed as lectors and acolytes, and it appears he was not opposed to both married priests and women deacons as well.

However, Francis's thinking seems to be to enlarge lay ministry before accepting women and more married men into ordained ministry. Such an approach makes eminent sense since he is overseeing a worldwide Church, and not every territory or jurisdiction holds the same attitude toward married or female clerics, and not every territory or jurisdiction can call on individuals with appropriate education or skills to be able to receive diaconal or priestly orders.

By January 2021, with his apostolic letter, *Spiritus Domini*, Francis modified canon 203 §1 to allow all laypersons, not only males, to be installed formally as lectors and acolytes. In that document, he noted that Paul VI had regulated the reception of lay ministries through his apostolic letter *Ministeria Quaedam*, issued *motu proprio* on August 17, 1972. Henceforth, even though some laymen had been installed as lectors and/or acolytes without the presumption they would be ordained as deacons, these lay ministries were now to be reclaimed as part of the Church's treasure. Francis underscored the distinction between the lay ministries of lector and acolyte, which had formerly been conferred as part of the *cursus honorum*, as steps toward priestly ordination. He wrote that "a doctrinal development has taken place in recent years which has highlighted how certain ministries instituted by the Church are based on the common condition of being baptized and the royal priesthood received in the Sacrament of Baptism." Furthermore, he emphasized the fact that these ministries are "essentially distinct from the ordained ministry received in the Sacrament of Orders."[46]

A few months after opening installation as lector and acolyte to all laypersons, Francis further expanded installed lay ministry. In May 2021, he established a new lay ministry, that of catechist, through his apostolic letter *Antiquum Ministerium*, which he issued *motu proprio*.[47] In this much longer document, he presents the argument for expanded lay ministry, which he details as a work of evangelization proper to the entire people of God, yet bounded by the restrictions necessary for adequate training and supervision and according to the needs of individual dioceses and eparchies.

The document also presents an intriguing sentence taken from Paul VI's *Ministeria Quaedam*:

> In addition to the ministries common to the entire Latin Church, nothing prevents Episcopal Conferences from asking the Apostolic See for the institution of others, which for particular reasons, they consider necessary or very useful in their own region. Among these are, for example, the offices of *Porter, Exorcist* and *Catechist*.[48]

Does the trajectory of thought in these three documents—Francis on lectors and acolytes, and on catechists; and Paul VI on the suppression of the minor orders—open or close possibilities for the restoration of women to the ordained diaconate? The three can be received as continuing the reception of Vatican II, which emphasized the people of God as both the constituency and the composition of the Church as served by the hierarchy. The three may also be intuited as a means of closing off or at least forestalling the restoration of women to the clerical state, despite increasing synodal calls to ordain women.

That synodal discussion can and even has moved beyond its established boundaries to include concepts that go beyond the development of doctrine to the extent that Rome has issued warnings in an attempt to rein in some processes. For example, recently the Vatican presented a "Declaration of the Holy See" about the German "Synodal Path," which has apparently headed in the direction of disagreeing with some doctrine (women priests) and moral teaching (homosexuality). In rather strong language, the unsigned Declaration states that the synod processes do not require ascent by the bishops, and in any event cannot take effect without agreement by the universal Church. In many respects the declaration is a warning to the German and perhaps other national synods to stay within the boundaries of the discussion as presented by the Synod Office.[49]

## Women Deacons and the Future[50]

The reception and affirmation of plenary and synodal processes depends on Rome. To preserve communion with the Bishop of Rome, the pope, any requests to change disciplinary practices can only be evaluated and decided upon at the papal level prior to their being requested at the national level and then implemented at the local (diocesan) level.

The essential argument on behalf of restoring women to the ordained diaconate, really one that is completely in line with the opening of the installed offices of lector and acolyte to women and the establishment of the new lay ministry of catechist, is that there is no doctrinal barrier to such restoration. That is, historical ordinations of women to the diaconate are documented, and the current restriction against ordaining women as deacons is a disciplinary matter.

The Vatican Library's holdings, along with those of several other European libraries, include manuscripts of liturgies known to have been used by bishops to ordain women as deacons within the sanctuary, during the Mass, in the presence of the clergy, through the imposition of hands by the Holy Spirit; they self-communicated from the chalice, the bishop placed a stole around their necks, and the bishop called them deacons.[51]

The diaconate is an office whose origins are found in scriptural passages specifically tied to the apostles' wish to expand their ministry after the death of Jesus. As Francis said to the assembled bishops, in

*[handwritten margin note: Irony of both cause + solution being in clericalism]*

2015, when he visited Saint Charles Borromeo Seminary in Philadelphia,

> In the early days of the Church, the Hellenists complained that their widows and orphans were not being well cared for. The apostles, of course, weren't able to handle this themselves, so they got together and came up with deacons. The Holy Spirit inspired them to create deacons.[52]

That the diaconate preceded the development of the priesthood is often overlooked, and throughout the first millennia of the Church, the diaconate grew and expanded to become an extremely powerful clerical caste. Concurrently, the custom of the *cursus honorum* took hold, so that the various ministries no longer existed as distinct and permanent offices, but rather were collapsed into a series of stages or steps toward priesthood.

Clerical tonsure, signifying entry into the clerical state, was followed by ordination to the minor orders of porter, lector, exorcist, and acolyte. These preceded ordination to the major orders of subdeacon, deacon, and priest. The accompanying tasks and duties of these offices were specifically tied to the celebration of the liturgy.

Along the way, individual status of the minor and major orders was lost and, by the time the Italian monk and canonist Gratian (1101–1159) was writing, one was rarely, if ever, permitted to be ordained as deacon unless he was destined to be ordained a priest. The *Decretum Gratani* collected some four thousand Church laws up to and including the decretals of the twelfth-century Lateran Council (1139). The *Decretum* undergird the *Decretals* of Gregory IX in 1234, which, in turn, formed the basis of the first part of Catholic canon law until the creation and codification of the 1917 Pio-Benedictine Code of Canon Law.

Those laws were all codified after the diaconate as a separate ministry had been subsumed into the *cursus honorum* and, thereby, apparently inextricably tied to the priesthood. The law regarding ordination appeared in 1983 as canon 1024, which stated that only males were validly ordained. That is, by 1983, law was making a doctrinal statement, and there was no distinction within canon 1024 between deacons and priests.

Since the 1983 Code, Rome repeatedly issued documents, most if not all emanating from the pen of Joseph Ratzinger, stating that women cannot be ordained as priests.[53] That is, validity, not liceity (or legitimacy) was legislated and further supported through three documents: the declaration *Inter Insigniores*, issued on October 15, 1976, by the Sacred Congregation for the Doctrine of the Faith with the approval of Pope Paul VI;[54] the apostolic letter *Ordinatio Sacerdotalis*, issued on May 22, 1994;[55] and the document "Concerning the Reply of the Congregation for the Doctrine of the Faith on the Teaching Contained in the apostolic letter, *Ordinatio Sacerdotalis*" (or *Dubium*), issued the following year on October 28, 1995,[56] as well as other documents throughout Ratzinger's term as prefect of the Congregation of the Doctrine of the Faith and as pope.

But, as Pope Benedict XVI ruled in 2009, the diaconate is not the priesthood. Benedict's apostolic letter *Omnium in Mentem*, issued *motu proprio* on October 26, 2009, added a third paragraph to canon 1009 of the revised 1983 Code of Canon Law:

> Those who are constituted in the order of the episcopate or the presbyterate receive the mission and capacity to act in the person of Christ the Head, whereas deacons are empowered to serve the People of God in the ministries of the liturgy, the word and charity.[57]

That is, the diaconate is not part of the priesthood.

\* attracted to historical and biblical arguments

# 4

## Conclusions

To where does all this lead? The question is genuine: Can the center hold? It is no secret that the tensions both inside and outside Vatican walls and chanceries around the world find two sides to the Catholic story—there is a split between those who follow the lead of Pope Francis and those who remain attached to Tridentine liturgies; between those who accept and those who do not accept the findings, the teachings, of the Second Vatican Council.

Can these two sides be reconciled? Catholic Social Teaching is specific in its tenets, as is the concept of synodality as recovered by Vatican II. Where does the confluence of these two rivers of Church teaching and thought leave women? Does it include or exclude women, either historically or in the present? Women represent the largest cadre of the periphery that Francis calls the center. What entrée does the periphery have to decision-making? How can Catholic Social Teaching and the concept of synodality combine to bring justice to women in the Church?

# CATHOLIC SOCIAL TEACHING

The trajectory of Catholic Social Teaching since Leo XIII's *Rerum Novarum* is one that demonstrates that, along with governments in developed countries, the Church has increasingly recognized the rights of the individuals who make up the periphery. While all Church documents are essentially an explication of gospel teaching, Vatican II forms a genuine line of demarcation in documents generally categorized as comprising Catholic Social Teaching.

Pre–Vatican II documents differ markedly in tenor and scope from those that followed the close of the council. What appears most readily is a movement of the writer closer to the individuals to whom the document is addressed. While the attitude of Francis toward the people of God and the hierarchy is markedly different from that of his two immediate predecessors, when we look beyond the writings of John Paul II and Benedict XVI, there are even more distinctions.

The papacy became markedly less regal, less detached, during the papacy of Paul VI, who, we must recall, lay in state in a simple cypress coffin more than a decade after he donated his papal tiara to the poor of the world. It was the recognition of world poverty discussed by the council fathers that led Paul to lay his tiara on the altar following the November 1964 celebration of a council Mass in the Byzantine-Slavic Rite. During nine weeks of debate at the council, many council members urged the Church to forgo "pomp and 'triumphal' clothing and ornament and embrace poverty."[1] That discussion is still taking place today.

Pope Paul VI's actions, joined with his words, set the Church on a simpler, some say more inclusive, course. The council documents clearly pointed to both inclusivity (although the term was not used) and a genuine call for application of the Church's social teaching in all areas of life. That the Church, internally, did not move as quickly as it advised the rest of the world to is testimony to the specter of clericalism still haunting the Catholic Church.

Clericalism, embedded in so many areas of Church life, collides with Catholic Social Teaching as it might be applied internally. Church membership is, doctrinally at least, equal for all. But lay members of the Church, be they religious or seculars, still find themselves on a different rung of the ladder of influence. Efforts to overcome the great clerical-lay divide are stymied by custom, tradition, and law, all wrapped around an ingrained memory of the problems of modernism, and they were understood at the beginning of the twentieth century, well before the Vatican Council, even before the truncated First Vatican Council (December 8, 1869, to October 20, 1870), which is perhaps best recalled as the council that defined papal infallibility. While the First Vatican Council was billed as an ecumenical council, invited Orthodox and Lutheran clerics did not attend.[2]

In 1907, nearly forty years after the close of Vatican I, Pius X's "Syllabus Condemning the Errors of the Modernists" appeared, supporting the notion that nothing in the Church is subject to development or change and that the Church is, in fact, immutable. The Oath against Modernism remained a requirement for some sixty years. While it was not rescinded, its use was replaced, in 1967, by the Profession of Faith of Paul VI, comprised of the Creed with the following final paragraph:

> I also firmly accept and retain each and every truth regarding the doctrine of faith and morals, whether solemnly defined by the Church or asserted and declared with the ordinary Magisterium, as well as those doctrines proposed by the same Magisterium, above all those which regard the mystery of the Holy Church of Christ, the Sacraments, the Sacrifice of the Mass, as well as the Primacy of the Roman Pontiff.[3]

The Profession of Faith affirms acceptance and belief in doctrines regarding faith and morals, as well as those regarding sacraments, papal primacy, and the Church itself. Because the Profession of Faith was promulgated following the close of Vatican II, this arguably means that its acceptance includes the acceptance of all the findings and recommendations of the council.

Beyond the findings and recommendations of the council, its underlying attitude is critical to assessing the ways in which Catholic Social Teaching has or has not been assimilated into Church thought and practice since the close of the council.

Admittedly, it takes many decades to assimilate the teachings of a council, and many more to overcome its improper reception. If Leo XIII's *Rerum Novarum* is a fruit of the Church's recognition of the needs of the world in the years following the close of Vatican I, during growing industrialization that threatened to reduce (or even actually reduced) persons to cogs in a metaphorical spinning wheel, then the appearance of the encyclical marks a fine point in Church history. In fact, *Rerum Novarum* marks a place in time when the Church began to side with the poor in the public sphere. It does not mark a place in time when "the Church," that is, the hierarchy, turned its gaze inward.

While industrialization promised improvements to the general standard of living for many individuals, fair employment standards were far from developed and the criticisms of *Rerum Novarum* did not seem to apply to the Church's internal organizations. If the life and dignity of the human person is a bedrock belief of Catholic Social Teaching, then the Church as a whole—the people of God and the hierarchy—must rethink policies regarding women that hinge on the statement that women cannot image Christ. Ontological equality does not presume denial of gender differences; it presumes that all are made in the image and likeness of God.

*Lumen Gentium*, the Dogmatic Constitution on the Church, appearing more than half a century after *Rerum Novarum*, asserts that all the people of God are "sharing a common dignity" and there is "in Christ and in the Church no inequality...'neither male nor female.'"[4] Solemnly promulgated by Pope Paul VI in November 1964—one week after he laid his tiara on the altar of the basilica—the document is the fruit of the highest level of Church, an ecumenical council. Every bishop, every pastor, every ordinary makes the Profession of Faith. Does every one of these men—and they are primarily, if not solely men—agree that women are equally human and made in the image and likeness of God?

If all clerics believed in the dignity of women, then their professed solidarity with the poor would focus on the women of the world for whom poverty of many descriptions is a pressing danger. As fire and drought join clear cutting and pollution, attacking the lives and livelihoods of thousands of women, they would be speaking out more forcefully about the care for God's creation. These same ordinaries would be finding space even in the conservative media they control to defend the planet, and by implication, the hundreds of thousands of women who suffer the tortures of war and general disregard for the environment daily.

Yet the fault line growing larger in various parts of the Church separates those for whom Catholic Social Teaching presents priorities they are willing to accept from those who follow a more secular agenda. The members of the hierarchy and their followers for whom *Rerum Novarum* is merely advisory and who ignore the reiteration of its themes in Paul VI's *Populorum Progressio* (March 26, 1967) and John Paul II's *Sollicitudo Rei Socialis* (December 30, 1987) are disagreeing with Church teaching in many ways. Importantly, they ignore John Paul II's call:

> I invite all to reflect and actively commit themselves to promoting the true development of peoples, as the prayer of the Mass for this intention states so well: "Father, you have given all peoples one common origin, and your will is to gather them as one family in yourself. Fill the hearts of all with the fire of your love, and the desire to ensure justice for all their brothers and sisters. By sharing the good things you give us, may we secure justice and equality for every human being, an end to all division and a human society built on love and peace."[5]

Can the Church recover its dedication to the call to family, community and, most of all, participation by all its members? The fraught discussions about who can create family will not end soon, but a Christian nonjudgmental attitude after the fact can be understood in the light of Catholic Social Teaching. That is, while it is highly unlikely that Church teaching on homosexual relationships will change, except considering overwhelming scientific advancement, there is every reason to extend Christian charity to different forms of family in the community. Similarly, persons in what are termed "irregular marriages" can and, in fact, must be respected as human persons despite the Church's inability to recognize the unions.

As for public participation by public figures in the sacramental life of the Church, it is equally unlikely that teachings on abortion, for example, will change, as in no way is the question of human life subject to the development of doctrine. But the failure of the Church to convince its members, and by extension the electorate, of doctrine in respect to these matters creates a conundrum for both politicians and bishops. The politician serves his voters; the duty of the bishop is not only to correct the politician but also teach the voters. Furthermore, given the mixture of laws in the United States and elsewhere, it is incumbent on bishops to define "life of the mother" exceptions clearly, so as to protect women for whom so-called double effect procedures would be lifesaving.[6]

The tragedy of misapplication of doctrine and maladaptation of Catholic Social Teaching creates a vacuum that sucks the life out of the poor and vulnerable. It cannot be overstated: the ignoring or overriding of Church teachings by individuals, corporations, and governments, as well as by Church institutions and organizations, ultimately damages the poor and vulnerable, for whom a preferential option is supposedly held. The root of the problem is the inability or unwillingness by any of these—persons, companies, nation-states, or the Church—to pay just wages. Both internal and external so-called healthy economies are required to render justice, but even within healthy economies, women—including Church employees—are too often underpaid and left without the fringe benefits often required by employment law.

For example, the parishes that refuse to pay female workers (e.g., the rectory cooks, secretaries, liturgy coordinators, social service managers) full-time salaries, while employing male workers (e.g., executive assistants, custodians, audio-video and social media technical support) at full salaries and benefits, are essentially stealing from the poor. Justice is not served in these and too many other situations.

In sum, the categories of traditional Catholic Social Teaching combine to underscore the bedrock of Catholic doctrine, that all persons have the right to be treated fairly and equally, and for them and their environs to be respected and protected. Unfortunately, there are more instances than not where women are left out of the mix, where women are not fully members of whatever situation or event taking place. There is every reason to recognize that, where the hierarchical Church implies or clergy state that women cannot image Christ, it and they are complicit in the worst kind of genocide. A suicidal Church cannot perdure.

# SYNODALITY

No matter how often the Church convenes in synods, the question of actual synod membership will hang over requests, decisions, and pronouncements emanating from them. When thinking of "cancel culture," perhaps one must include women as the first to be canceled.[7]

In June 2022, at the close of the initial phase of the Synod on Synodality, many dioceses in the United States published their reports, including the Archdiocese of San Francisco. Led by conservative Archbishop Salvatore J. Cordileone, the archdiocese reported nine virtual synod meetings held via Zoom and sixteen in-person sessions hosted by parishes. The report includes the following:

> During the scripture reflection sharing, a woman (40's) was dominating the time with a women's rights position. The group listened respectfully to her, and during the break a deacon who was co-leading the session offered his thoughts. As the topic listening/sharing portion began, a man (40's) at her table took a leadership position. He asked the table to

begin with something positive. He recognized the woman's agenda and lovingly offered a way to balance the discussion and demonstrate a synodal spirit.[8]

Such is an example of "mansplaining," all too common in Church circles.

The San Francisco report, like many from dioceses led by bishops in the anti-Francis, anti–Vatican II camp, did not distinguish between what it termed "the Church's authoritative teachings" and matters of policy or discipline. For example, the San Francisco report implied that questioning the Church's stance on care for creation and the ordination of married men exemplified questioning authoritative teachings.[9]

As other reports appeared, there was little evidence that dioceses have followed the clear direction of the Synod Office's *Vademecum*:

> As a model of transparency, the members of the drafting team as well as the process of synthesizing the feedback can be made known to all. It is strongly recommended that the synthesis be made public once it has been drafted, as a touchstone for the journey of the diocese along the path of synodality. As much as possible, opportunities can be given to the People of God to review and respond to the content of the diocesan synthesis before it is officially sent to the episcopal conference.[10]

Early on, the United States Conference of Catholic Bishops (USCCB) reported that some 95 percent of dioceses had filed their reports, but few, if any, were posted for commentary in advance of the USCCB June 2022 deadline. Yet many diocesan reports pointed to clericalism and the lack of women in leadership as troubling, even problematic in relation to the evangelical mission of the Church.[11] For example, the Diocese of Buffalo, which includes eight counties in western New York State, reported that "the abuse scandal [and] the lack of respect for women as manifested in an all-male clergy" caused declining Church attendance and membership.[12]

Reports from the first part of the Synod on Synodality, both in the United States and in many countries around the world, repeat the same theme: clericalism is a scourge on the Church, and women are not respected or included in leadership. For example, the report from France, the "eldest daughter of the Church," reflects the approximations of Church membership there: from 41 percent to 88 percent of the population (between 27 and 58 million people). That is, while 88 percent of the population is nominally Catholic, only 41 percent consider themselves as actual Church members. The synod process demonstrated why. Respondents were dissatisfied with the place of women in the Church and stressed that their sufferings and expectations must be recognized.[13] The report prepared by the Catholic Bishops' Conference of England and Wales shared much the same findings, recognizing that women were a "silenced, unrecognized majority...excluded from leadership and ministry."[14]

Many dioceses in the Republic of Ireland asked for women to be ordained as deacons, noting the declining numbers of priests.[15]

As noted, Australia moved forward with its Fifth Plenary Council.[16] The following article was finally approved:

> Article 4. That, should the universal law of the Church be modified to authorize the diaconate for women, the Plenary Council recommends that the Australian Bishops examine how best to implement it in the context of the Church in Australia.[17]

Elsewhere, synodal discussion does not appear to be distinguishing matters of discipline from those of doctrine. The long German synodal process produced results such that it received a Vatican warning that Rome would make determinations, all in keeping with Church teaching.[18]

As the national synod reports arrived in Rome, they were synthesized into another document in preparation for yet another round of discussions, all leading to the October 2023 synod meeting of some three hundred representatives in Rome. While women have never been able to vote during synods, at least one woman, the Xaverian Synod of Bishops' Under-Secretary, Sister Nathalie Becquart, is expected to have a vote. She has defined synodality as a way of being Church rooted in the model given by the "Council" of Jerusalem (Acts 15) that "emphasizes the equal dignity of all the baptized."[19]

Contemporary synod processes and reports demonstrate the current understanding of "synodality" as presented by Becquart and by the International Theological Commission before her. The key understanding is that the synod is a meeting of the disciples of Jesus. The question presented by Francis is, Who are the disciples?

Throughout history, as the Church grew in membership and its bureaucracy developed concomitantly, synods increasingly became meetings of clerics and then only of bishops. Paul VI, who established the formal Synod of Bishops in 1965, convened four before his death in 1978. His successor, John Paul II, promulgated his apostolic exhortation on catechesis and youth following the fourth of Paul VI's synods.

Both John Paul II and Benedict XVI held several synods, both Ordinary and Extraordinary, and Francis has so far held three major synods leading up to his Synod on Synodality, which might have been more clearly titled a Synod on Ecclesiology.

What has become evident during the years of Francis's papacy is that he is unafraid to open discussion on delicate matters. The Synod on the Family (2014–2015) presaged the discussions to come, discussions that can threaten to fracture some Church alliances even as they strengthen others. Controversies that arose during and after those synod meetings have continued throughout Francis's papacy, most (if not all) related to objective worthiness for reception of Communion.

More recent discussions focus on other cases where individuals are deemed, sometimes publicly, as unworthy to receive Communion. In every instance, whether general discussions about divorced and remarried persons and others in what are referred to as "irregular unions," or about individuals involved in political discussion regarding abortion laws, tension appears between those who seek to bar persons from the sacrament and those who seek to ameliorate their situations. The "hardliners" too often align themselves with other groups and individuals who oppose reforms presented to the Church by Francis, specifically persons who are attached to the Tridentine Mass and reject the liturgical modifications of Vatican II.

These individuals and groups, many concentrated in the United States and influenced (or involved with) the various media outlets owned and operated by Eternal Word Television Network (EWTN), are in abject denial of the primacy of the pope when he speaks on matters with which they disagree. They both openly and not so openly deride Francis's efforts at synodality as they have evolved throughout his papacy. Their attacks have been so virulent that Francis included the media network with others as doing "the work of the devil."[20]

Other outlets owned by EWTN, which is quite probably the world's largest religious media outlet, include the *National Catholic Register* newspaper and Catholic News Agency.[21] The latter is often confused with the Catholic News Service, which the U.S. Conference of Catholic Bishops gave over to another relatively conservative outlet, Our Sunday Visitor, in 2022.[22]

Concomitantly, internal forces in the Vatican have too often attempted to block or stall Francis's initiatives. The publication of the apostolic constitution *Praedicate Evangelium* on the ninth anniversary of Francis's accession to the papacy, March 19, 2022, is an example of passive aggressiveness within the Vatican. The document was reportedly stalled, some say by the lawyers, some say by the translators, for many months after Francis's group of cardinal advisors, the C-9, completed their work. The document was reportedly drafted by the end of 2019.[23] It was first published only in Italian, the official English translation appeared on the Vatican website in late June 2022.

A large part of the problem was that, throughout his pontificate, Francis has had another pope literally in his backyard. When Benedict XVI resigned, he did not repair to Germany, despite rumors that he planned to retire to live there with his older brother, Msgr. George Ratzinger. Benedict instead displaced a group of Spanish contemplative nuns, revamping the monastery in the Vatican Gardens as his own residence.[24]

While Benedict is no longer as alert or intellectually active as when he first retired, the fact of his being in the Vatican as *pope emeritus* (a title he chose for himself) encourages his cadre of followers, including individuals who can or at least attempt to influence Vatican documents and affairs.[25] Hence, despite the fact that Francis has never digressed from any doctrine, there are segments of society claiming Church membership who deny Francis's authority as pope.

For this reason, as well as for the content of synod final documents and ensuing apostolic exhortations by Francis, the growing gap between the groups best understood as pro- and anti-Vatican II continues to grow. Whether synodality can close that gap, or even encourage opposing groups to converse civilly, remains to be seen as the results of the Synod on Synodality continue to unfold.

Prior synods, particularly that on Young People in 2018, evidenced Francis's interest, if not that of the entire hierarchy, in listening to more than just bishops in synods. What he heard then is what he hears now: the young people involved in that synod spoke openly and freely about the fact that women were essentially eliminated from any positions of leadership, whether managerial or ministerial, because of their gender. Francis responded by admitting that when the Church was "overly fearful and tied to its structures," it could not accommodate the criticisms levied regarding the way women are treated by and within the Church.

One wonders if the naysayers would understand what the pope was saying any better if the name of another peripheral group was inserted: indigenous persons, people of color, the handicapped, and the elderly. The list is endless, for the periphery is large.

Francis addressed the needs of the periphery well when, in 2019, he convened the Amazon Synod with an *Instrumentum laboris* (working document) that invited the synod members to find ways to evangelize the peoples of the Amazon region. The preparation for the synod began in 2014 with the creation of the Pan-Amazon Ecclesial Network (REPAM) and its velocity increased with the release of Francis's encyclical on the environment, *Laudato Si'*, in 2015.

The Amazon Synod itself was an example of synodality, and the members certainly made their interests known. Francis's actions following the release of his apostolic exhortation *Querida Amazonia* included both surprises and omissions of hoped-for changes. He had clearly said that his own document needed to be read in tandem with the Amazon Synod's Final Document, which, in and of itself, was an affirmation of synodality. The Final Document called explicitly for married priests and implicitly for women deacons and, in the months following the publication of *Querida Amazonia*, successive apostolic letters presented the Church with the possibility of women formally installed as lectors and acolytes, and the whole Church recovering the ministry of catechist as a formal, installed ministry for both men and women. He also emphasized the need, or at least the increased possibility for, parish life coordinators as allowed for by canon 517.2. This last point is important because it placed the vocation to lead a parish outside the vocation to clerical status, without eliminating the possibility of them being conjoined.

And so, the Church, enjoying increasing possibilities for lay ministry, embarked on the Synod on Synodality. Some parishes, some dioceses, some national episcopal conferences took the challenge seriously and openly conducted synodal conversations; some others, perhaps, missed the point; while others ignored the call completely.

# WOMEN IN THE CHURCH

Whether or not synodal conversations result in changes to Church discipline or developments in doctrine can only be judged by history. As for the place of women in the Church, the conversation approaches both discipline and doctrine. Restoring women to the ordained diaconate is a matter of discipline, as demonstrated by copious research. The question regarding women deacons is not whether women can be ordained as deacons, but whether they should be ordained. Does the Church need women to be ordained as deacons? That question is for the whole Church to answer. Today, the synodal answer is yes.

For many convergent reasons, the response to the need for women deacons in various areas of the Church is confused, purposefully or not, with the question of women priests. There is sparse historical evidence of the ordinations of women as priests. Often, epigraphical evidence of women deacons performing priestly functions is mistaken as evidence of women priests. It is important not to confuse or conjoin the two discussions—those regarding women deacons and those regarding women priests—because for the present, the Church has settled the question of women priests as a doctrinal matter. There is no doctrinal statement, neither historically nor contemporaneously, about women deacons. There are only various medieval legal documents forbidding continuation of the practice of ordaining women as deacons.

The debates about women clergy, however, cast light on the disciplinary discussion about ordaining more married men as priests. Current practice allows that a married man may be ordained, as deacon or priest, but an ordained man may not marry. There is little modern tradition to support ordination or consecration of married men as bishops. But to have a married priest implies a priest who engages in sexual relations, thereby raising the specter of his becoming impure and therefore unable to offer the sacrifice of the Mass. The received superstition about women's impurity, clearly attached to menstruation but extended to any woman at any time, extends to making men who touch women impure.

The notion of impurity is connected to both issues: married priests and women deacons, each at least an implicit request of the Amazon Synod and of local, regional, and national synods since then. No doubt a major part of the problem regarding women deacons is the questions about their historical tasks and duties.

When Francis agreed to institute a commission on women deacons at the request of the May 2016 meeting of the International Union of Superiors General (UISG), he specifically noted his interest in what functions women deacons performed. The sisters had noted that they performed all the tasks and duties of ordained deacons, particularly in developing parts of the world, asking why, then, could they not be ordained? But, before addressing this question of women deacons, he noted two important points that he addressed in ensuing years:

the need for more women in management roles at every level of the Church, and the need to address the danger of clericalism.[26]

Without doubt, he was correct. Clericalism, that is, the assumption of all control coupled with a superior attitude by clerics, is indeed the scourge he names. Very soon after he became pope, Francis presented the need for women to have "a more incisive presence for women in the Church." He since repeated that call, directly in 2015, in speaking with the UISG sisters in 2016, and again in 2020.[27]

The "more incisive presence" so far has been the increased inclusion of women in curial offices and, more recently, as actual members of dicasteries. These appointments are the result of *Praedicate Evangelium* and do indeed help the Church preach the gospel value that women are indeed equal to, if not the same as, men. That is, competent women can also attain offices previously held only by men, including those that include managerial supervision and/or oversight of clerics. While the contemporary societies of developed nations increasingly recognize and accept the competence of women, the clerical caste, particularly within the Vatican, still demonstrates difficulty with the notion of women in managerial positions.

Various cultures have various ways of assimilating women, but the restoration of women to ordained service as deacons seems to be acceptable, and in fact, necessary. The argument that restoring women as deacons requires doctrinal development ignores the notion of the living tradition. In opening the Synod on the Family in 2015, Francis said the deposit of faith is not a museum, but a "living spring" that illuminates the "deposit of life." He there explained the concept of synodality: the examination of tradition in the light of doctrine, to reinsure the Church's fidelity to its beliefs, as below:

> The Synod is rather an *ecclesial expression*, i.e., the Church that journeys together to understand reality with the eyes of faith and with the heart of God; it is the Church that questions herself with regard to her fidelity to the *deposit of faith*, which does not represent for the Church a museum to view, nor just something to safeguard, but is a living spring

from which the Church drinks, to satisfy the thirst of, and illuminate the *deposit of life*.[28]

By affirming the positive nature of ecclesial growth, Francis affirms the principle of safeguarding doctrine. In speaking further about ecclesial development, he often cites Saint Vincent of Lérins, whose words demonstrate his hope for the Church, for a synodal Church: *ut annis scilicet consolidetur, dilatetur tempore, sublimetur aetate* (that it may be consolidated over the years, developed with time, and deepened with age).

Francis's notion of a constantly developing ecclesiology is clear: by repeatedly citing Saint Vincent in *Laudato Si'* in 2015, by amending the Catechism on the death penalty in 2017, in his closing address to the Amazon Synod in 2019, and when launching the Synod on Synodality in September 2021, he argued both implicitly and explicitly against the rigidity of those who deny the changes proposed by and advanced following Vatican II. He is not afraid of change.

The hopes of women in the Church, however, cannot depend on one man. Popes come and go. Francis's successor will undoubtably inherit a Church where clericalism is rampant, where clerics claim priority within the Roman Curia and in curias around the world. While the questions of restoring women to all clerical orders continue to be considered jointly, that is, while the question continues to be not about restoring women to the ordained diaconate but rather about women being a suitable "subject" of holy orders, the circular arguments will continue. In other words, the assertion that you cannot ordain a woman as a deacon because you cannot ordain a woman a priest ignores both history and sacramental theology. Any person is eligible for any sacrament, unless impeded by divine or ecclesiastical law. So long as the circular arguments continue, the assertion that women are impeded by both divine and ecclesiastical law from ordination solidifies the understanding that women cannot be ordained as deacons.

But the treatment of women as equal persons, both within and without Church settings and employment, goes beyond questions of ordination. Justice, whether through the lens of Catholic Social Teaching, or as discussed in synod, is a touchstone of all gospel teachings.

Catholic Social Teaching requires humane and respectful treatment of persons and of the environment. To disrespect the latter is to disrespect the former. Synodality requires patient and respectful listening to all persons, whether those in power or those on the periphery. Incorporating women fully into the Church and its structures requires a cleansing of clericalism from all areas of society and acceptance of a deep recognition that all are made in the image and likeness of God, that all are icons of the living Christ.

Not moving forward, the Church suffers, moving in a downward spiral, and the center will not hold.

confused by "icon" language

# APPENDIX I

# Papal and Vatican Documents

*Rerum Novarum* (On the Condition of Labor)—Leo XIII, 1891.

*Quadragesimo Anno* (After Forty Years)—Pius XI, 1931.

*Mater et Magistra* (Christianity and Social Progress)—John XXIII, 1961.

*Pacem in Terris* (Peace on Earth)—John XXIII, 1963.

*Gaudium et Spes* (Pastoral Constitution on the Church in the Modern World)—Second Vatican Council, 1965.

*Dignitatis Humanae* (Declaration on Religious Freedom)—Second Vatican Council, 1965.

*Populorum Progressio* (On the Development of Peoples)—Paul VI, 1967.

*Octogesima Adveniens* (A Call to Action)—Paul VI, 1971.

*Evangelii Nuntiandi* (Evangelization in the Modern World)—Paul VI, 1975.

*Laborem Exercens* (On Human Work)—John Paul II, 1981.

*Sollicitudo Rei Socialis* (On Social Concern)—John Paul II, 1987.

The Church and Racism: Towards a More Fraternal Society—Pontifical Council for Justice and Peace, 1989.

*Centesimus Annus* (The Hundredth Year)—John Paul II, 1991.

*Veritatis Splendor* (The Splendor of Truth)—John Paul II, 1993.

*Evangelium Vitae* (The Gospel of Life)—John Paul II, 1995.

*Dignitas Personae* (The Dignity of a Person)—Congregation for the Doctrine of the Faith, 1998.

*Ecclesia in America* (The Church in America)—John Paul II, 1999.

*Fides et Ratio* (Faith and Reason)—John Paul II, 1998.

Doctrinal Note on Some Questions Regarding the Participation of Catholics in Political Life—Congregation for the Doctrine of the Faith, 2002.

Compendium of the Social Doctrine of the Church—Pontifical Council for Justice and Peace, 2004.

*Deus Caritas Est* (God Is Love)—Benedict XVI, 2005.

*Sacramentum Caritatis* (The Eucharist as the Source and Summit of the Church's Life and Mission)—Benedict XVI, 2007 (especially paragraphs 47, 49, 82–84, and 88–92).

*Caritas in Veritate* (Charity in Truth)—Benedict XVI, 2009.

*Evangelii Gaudium* (The Joy of the Gospel)—Francis, 2013.

*Laudato Si'* (On Care for Our Common Home)—Francis, 2015.

*Querida Amazonia* (Beloved Amazon)—Francis, 2020.

*Fratelli Tutti* (On Fraternity and Social Friendship)—Francis, 2020.

*Praedicate Evangelium* (On the Roman Curia and Its Service to the Church and to the World)—Francis, 2022.

# APPENDIX II

# Synods of Bishops

## ORDINARY GENERAL ASSEMBLIES OF THE SYNOD OF BISHOPS

1. Revision of the Code of Canon Law (September 29 to October 29, 1967). Documents: Institution of the International Theological Commission, and *Ratio Fundamentalis Institutionis Sacerdotalis.*

2. Ministerial Priesthood; Justice in the World (September 30 to November 6, 1971). Documents on Justice in the World and on the Ministerial Priesthood.

3. Evangelization of the Contemporary World (September 27 to October 26, 1974). Documents: Declaration of Synodal Fathers, and Paul VI's apostolic exhortation *Evangelii Nuntiandi.*

4. Catechesis in Our Time, Especially of Children and Youth (September 30 to October 29, 1977). Document: John Paul II's apostolic exhortation *Catechesi Tradendae.*

5. The Christian Family (September 26–October 25, 1980). Document: John Paul II's apostolic exhortation *Familiaris Consortio*.

6. Reconciliation and Penance in the Pastoral Mission of the Church (September 29–October 20, 1983). Document: John Paul II's apostolic exhortation *Reconciliatio et Paenitentia*.

7. Vocation and Mission of the Laity in the Church and in the World 20 Years after Vatican Council II (October 1–30, 1987). Document: John Paul II's apostolic exhortation *Christifedeles Laici*.

8. Formation of Priests in Contemporary Society (October 1–28, 1990). Document: John Paul II's apostolic exhortation *Pastores Dabo Vobis*.

9. Consecrated Life and Its Function in the Church and in the World (October 2–29, 1995). Document: John Paul II's apostolic exhortation *Vita Consecrata*.

10. The Bishop: Servant of the Gospel of Jesus Christ for the Hope of the World.

11. The Eucharist: Source and Summit of the Life and Mission of the Church.

12. The Word of God in the Life and the Mission of the Church.

13. The New Evangelization for the Transmission of the Christian Faith.

14. The Vocation and the Mission of the Family in the Church and in the contemporary World (October 4–25, 2015).

15. Young People, the Faith, and Vocational Discernment (October 3–28, 2018).

16. For a Synodal Church: Communion, Participation, and Mission (October 2023).

# GENERAL EXTRAORDINARY ASSEMBLIES OF THE SYNOD OF BISHOPS

1. Cooperation of Episcopal Conferences with the Holy See and among Themselves (September 11 to October 28, 1968). Documents: Message to Priests and Final Declaration.

2. Commemoration, Evaluation, and Promotion of Vatican Council II on the Twentieth Anniversary of Its Conclusion (November 25 to December 8, 1985). Documents: Message to Christians and Final Report of the Synod.

3. The Pastoral Challenges of the Family in the Context of Evangelization (October 5–14, 2014).

# SPECIAL ASSEMBLIES OF THE SYNOD OF BISHOPS

1. Special Synod of the Bishops of the Low Countries: The Church's Pastoral Care in Holland in the Present Situation (January 14–31, 1980). Final Document of the Special Synod.

2. Special Assembly for Europe: We Are Witnesses of Christ Who Has Delivered Us (November 28 to December 14, 1991).

3. Synod of Bishops Special Assembly for Africa: Africa and Its Mission of Evangelization toward the Year 2000: You Will Be My Witnesses (April 10–May 8, 1994). Document: Apostolic Exhortation "Ecclesia in Africa" (September 14, 1995).

4. Synod of Bishops Special Assembly for Lebanon: Christ Is Our Hope; Renewed by His Spirit, in Solidarity, We Witness to His Love (November 26–December 14, 1995). Document: Apostolic Exhortation, "A New Hope for Lebanon" (May 10, 1997).

5. Synod of Bishops Special Assembly for America: Encounter with the Living Jesus Christ, the Way to Conversion, Communion and Solidarity in America (November 16– December 12, 1997). Document: Apostolic Exhortation "Ecclesia in America" (January 22, 1999).

6. Synod of Bishops Special Assembly for Asia: Jesus Christ the Savior and His Mission of Love and Service in Asia; "That They May Have Life, and That They May Have It in Abundance" (April 19–May 14, 1998). Document: Apostolic Exhortation "Ecclesia in Asia" (November 6, 1999).

7. Synod of Bishop Special Assembly for Oceania: Jesus Christ and the Peoples of Oceania; To Walk His Way, Tell His Truth, Live His Life (November 22–February 12, 1998).

8. Synod of Bishops Second Special Assembly for Europe: Jesus Christ Living in His Church, Source of Hope for Europe (October 1–23, 1999).

9. Second Special Assembly for Africa. The Church in Africa at the Service of Reconciliation, Justice and Peace (October 4–25, 2009).

10. Special Assembly for the Middle East: The Catholic Church in the Middle East: Communion and Witness (October 10–24, 2010).

11. Special Assembly of the Synod of Bishops for the Pan-Amazon Region (October 6–27, 2019).

# Notes

## 1. CATHOLIC SOCIAL TEACHING

1. Pope Pius X, *Sacrorum Antistitum* (September 1, 1910), https://www.vatican.va.

2. Pope Pius X, *Pascendi Dominci Gregis* (September 8, 1907), https://www.vatican.va.

3. Decree of the Holy Office *Lamentabili Sane* (July 3, 1907), approved by Pope Pius X, https://www.papalencyclicals.net.

4. Pope Leo XIII, *Rerum Novarum* (May 15, 1891), https://www.vatican.va. The translators note to this section reads, "The title sometimes given to this encyclical, *On the Condition of the Working Classes*, is therefore perfectly justified. A few lines after this sentence, the Pope gives a more comprehensive definition of the subject of *Rerum novarum*. We are using it as a title."

5. María Paz Herrero Lorenzo, *Los Milagros de San Isidro: Códice de Juan Díacono* (Maria Paz Herrero Lorenzo, 1988). Isidore was canonized on March 12, 1522, along with Saints Ignatius of Loyola, Francis Xavier, Teresa of Ávila, and Philip Neri.

6. See *Lumen Gentium* 32, citing Rom 12:4–5; Eph 4:5; Gal 3:28; and Col 3:11. See also *Code of Canons of the Eastern Churches*, can. 11.

7.   Anthony M. Annett, *Cathonomics: How Catholic Tradition Can Create a More Just Economy* (Washington, DC: Georgetown University Press, 2022), 13.

8.   For example, in May 2021, Facebook removed the unofficial Catholic website LifeSiteNews for violating its policies regarding the coronavirus. See Jack Jenkins, "Facebook Removes Faith-Based Website for 'Misleading' Coronavirus Information," *The Washington Post* (May 7, 2021), https://www.washingtonpost.com.

9.   Annett, *Cathonomics*, 276–78.

10.   *Laudato Si'* 1. Citing "Canticle of the Creatures," in Regis J. Armstrong, *Francis of Assisi: Early Documents*, vol. 1 (Hyde Park, NY: New City Press, 1999), 113–14.

11.   Deloitte, "The Turning Point: A New Economic Climate in the United States," https://www2.deloitte.com/content/dam/Deloitte/us/Documents/about-deloitte/us-the-turning-point-a-new-economic-climate-in-the-united-states-january-2022.pdf, citing World Meteorological Organization (WMO), *WMO Atlas of Mortality and Economic Losses From Weather, Climate, and Water Extremes (1970–2019)*, WMO, no. 1267, 2021.

12.   Deloitte, "The Turning Point," citing National Oceanic and Atmospheric Administration (NOAA), *Assessing the U.S. Climate in 2021*, sourced from NOAA, 2022.

13.   See https://www.climate.gov/news-features/understanding-climate/climate-change-global-temperature#:~:text=According%20to%20NOAA's%202020%20Annual,more%20than%20twice%20that%20rate.

14.   On August 4, 2017, the administration of U.S. President Donald Trump advised the United Nations of its intent to withdraw from the Paris Agreement as soon as it was eligible to do so, in November 2020. President Joseph Biden signed an executive order to rejoin the agreement on his first day in office, January 20, 2021.

15.   *Roe v. Wade*, 410 U.S. 113 (1973) was overturned by the Supreme Court in *Dobbs v. Jackson Women's Health* Org., 142 S. Ct. 2228 (2022).

16. Lisa Lerer, "When Joe Biden Voted to Let States Overturn *Roe v. Wade*," *The New York Times*, March 29, 2019.

17. A few U.S. bishops supported Cordileone's move, and some joined in banning Pelosi from Communion within their (arch) dioceses, including Joseph Naumann (Kansas City, KS), Donald Hying (Madison, WI), Samuel Aquila (Denver), Joseph Strickland (Tyler, TX), James Conley (Lincoln, NE), Robert Vasa (Santa Rosa, CA), Michael Barber (Oakland, CA), Paul Coakley (Oklahoma City), Thomas Paprocki (Springfield, IL), David Ricken (Green Bay, WI), Liam Carey (Baker, OR), Thomas Daly (Spokane, WA), Michael Olson (Fort Worth, TX), James Wall (Gallup, NM). There are some 433 active and retired Catholic diocesan bishops and eparchs in the United States.

18. The report was approved by 64 of 69 voting members.

19. Charles W. Norris, "The Papal Commission on Birth Control—Revisited," *The Linacre Quarterly* 80, no. 1 (2013): 8–16; Michael Dummett, "The Documents of the Papal Commission on Birth Control," *New Blackfriars*, 50, no. 585 (1969): 241–50.

20. The Seventh Lambeth Conference (1930) allowed "in those cases where there is such a clearly felt moral obligation to limit or avoid parenthood, and where there is a morally sound reason for avoiding complete abstinence, the Conference agrees that other methods may be used, provided that this is done in the light of the same Christian principles." J. J. Coyne, "The Coming Lambeth Conference," *The Tablet* (December 7, 1957), 4. See also the Anglican Communion Document Library, https://www.anglicancommunion.org/resources/document-library.aspx?author=Lambeth+Conference&year=1930.

21. Benedict XVI, encyclical letter *Deus Caritas Est* (December 25, 2005), no. 23.

22. Benedict XVI, *Deus Caritas Est*, citing Saint Ambrose, *De officiis ministrorum*, II, 28, 140: PL 16, 141, https://www.vatican.va.

23. United States Catholic Bishops, *Economic Justice for All: Pastoral Letter on Catholic Social Teaching and the U.S. Economy*, 1986, https://www.usccb.org/upload/economic_justice_for_all.pdf.

24. John Paul II, *Familiaris Consortio* (November 22, 1981), no. 24.

25. John Paul II, *Familiaris Consortio* 23.

26. John Paul's words may have helped. The UN's Convention on the Elimination of All Forms of Discrimination Against Women (1979), signed by 189 countries, includes suffrage as a basic right.

27. UN Women, *Global Fact Sheet 2019–2020*, https://www .unwomen.org/sites/default/files/Headquarters/Attachments/ Sections/Library/Publications/2019/POWW-2019-Fact-sheet -Global-en.pdf.

28. This passage is read at Mass in Cycle B on the Twenty-First Sunday of Ordinary Time and on Tuesday, the Thirtieth Week of Ordinary Time, and at other times in the liturgical year.

29. United Nations Commission on the Status of Women, *Report on the Sixty-Sixth Session* (March 26, 2021, and March 14–25, 2022), New York: United Nations, accessed August 1, 2022, see https://www .unwomen.org/en/csw/csw66-2022.

30. *Beijing Declaration and Platform for Action*, The Fourth World Conference on Women, September 4–15, 1995, https://www.un.org/ womenwatch/daw/beijing/pdf/BDPfA%20E.pdf.

31. Church organizations are not alone in the mistreatment and disrespect of female employees.

32. An analysis of these points can be found in *Women Engaging the Catholic Social Tradition: Solidarity toward the Common Good*, ed. Erin M. Brigham and Mary Johnson, SNDdeN (Mahwah, NJ: Paulist Press, 2022).

# 2. SYNODALITY

1. The Synod of Bishops website for virtual meetings, http:// synodmeetings.com.

2. International Theological Commission, "Synodality in the Life and Mission of the Church" (March 2, 2018) 3, citing G. Lampe, *A Patristic Greek Lexicon* (Oxford: Clarendon Press, 1968), 1334–35. See

also Rafael Luciani, *Synodality: A New Way of Proceeding in the Church* (Mahwah, NJ: Paulist Press, 2022).

3. International Theological Commission, "Synodality in the Life and Mission of the Church" 25, citing Cyprian, *Epistula* 14, 4 (CSEL III, 2, p. 512).

4. International Theological Commission, "Synodality in the Life and Mission of the Church" 27, citing Apostolic Canons (Mansi, *Sacrorum Conciliorum nova et amplissima collectio* I, 35).

5. International Theological Commission, "Synodality in the Life and Mission of the Church" 39. Here the ITC cites its own earlier document: International Theological Commission, "*Sensus Fidei* in the Life of the Church" (2014), no. 41.

6. See Synod of Bishops, http://secretariat.synod.va, accessed August 2, 2022.

7. International Theological Commission, "Synodality in the Life and Mission of the Church" 40.

8. *La seconda cosa è il preannuncio, che Noi stessi siamo lieti di darvi, della istituzione, auspicata da questo Concilio, d'un Sinodo di Vescovi, che, composto di Presuli, nominati per la maggior parte dalle Conferenze Episcopali, con la Nostra approvazione, sarà convocato, secondo i bisogni della Chiesa, dal Romano Pontefice, per Sua consultazione e collaborazione, quando, per il bene generale della Chiesa ciò sembrerà a Lui opportuno. Riteniamo superfluo aggiungere che questa collaborazione dell'Episcopato deve tornare di grandissimo giovamento alla Santa Sede e a tutta la Chiesa, e in particolare modo potrà essere utile al quotidiano lavoro della Curia Romana, a cui dobbiamo tanta riconoscenza per il suo validissimo aiuto, e di cui, come i Vescovi nelle loro diocesi, così anche Noi abbiamo permanentemente bisogno per le Nostre sollecitudini apostoliche. Notizie e norme saranno quanto prima portate a conoscenza di questa assemblea. Noi non abbiamo voluto privarci dell'onore e del piacere di farvi questa succinta comunicazione per attestarvi ancora una volta personalmente la Nostra fiducia, la Nostra stima e la Nostra fraternità. Mettiamo sotto la protezione di Maria santissima questa bella e promettente novità.* See https://www .vatican.va. (Available only in Italian, Latin, and Portuguese.)

9. Pope Paul VI, Apostolic Letter (issued *motu proprio*) *Apostolica Sollicitudo*, establishing the Synod of Bishops for the Universal Church (September 15, 1965), no. XII, https://www.vatican.va.

10. Pope Paul VI, *Apostolica Sollicitudo* VII.

11. Synod of Bishops, III Extraordinary General Assembly, "The Pastoral Challenges of the Family in the Context of Evangelization, *Instrumentum Laboris*," 2014, https://www.vatican.va.

12. Synod of Bishops, III Extraordinary General Assembly, "The Pastoral Challenges of the Family in the Context of Evangelization, Preparatory Document," 2013, https://www.vatican.va.

13. Synod of Bishops, III Extraordinary General Assembly, "The Pastoral Challenges of the Family in the Context of Evangelization, *Instrumentum Laboris*," 2014, Introduction.

14. Bill Chappell, "Pope Francis Discusses Gay Catholics; 'Who Am I To Judge?,'" *National Public Radio, WNYC*, "The Two-Way" (July 29, 2013), https://www.npr.org/sections/thetwo-way/.

15. Pope Francis, *The Name of God Is Mercy* (New York: Random House, 2016).

16. Joshua J. McElwee, "Pope Francis Confirms Finality of Ban on Ordaining Women Priests," *National Catholic Reporter* (November 1, 2016), https://www.ncronline.org.

17. Francis, Post-synodal Apostolic Exhortation *Amoris Laetitia*, (March 19, 2016), no. 3.

18. Francis, *Amoris Laetitia* 305.

19. Francis, *Amoris Laetitia*, n351.

20. Luke Hansen, "Archbishop Durocher: Address Violence against Women, Empower Women in the Church," *America* (October 23, 2015), https://www.americamagazine.org.

21. The bishops of Canada meet and discuss issues prior to their representatives departing for synods. Durocher's intervention can be taken as a comment of the entire Conference of Catholic Bishops of Canada. Other bishops, including San Diego Cardinal Robert McElroy, have voiced the same fact. See Joshua J. McElroy, "On Catholic Women Deacons, San Diego's McElroy Is 'in Favor of It,'" *National Catholic Reporter* (October 28, 2019), https://www.ncronline.org.

22. Francis, Apostolic Constitution *Episcopalis Communio,* on the Synod of Bishops (September 15, 2018), http://www.synod.va. Two papal documents are of higher level: a papal bull makes an official declaration and announcement, an encyclical addresses Church doctrine.

23. See, for example, Paul VI's discourse at the start of the first synod, *Disorso di Paolo VI all'inizio dei lavori nell'aula sinodale* (September 20, 1967), https://www.vatican.va.

24. Paul VI, *Disorso di Paolo VI* 1.

25. Francis, Apostolic Constitution *Episcopalis Communio* (September 15, 2018), no. 5, citing Francis, Apostolic Exhortation *Evangelii Gaudium* (November 24, 2013), no. 119, https://www.vatican.va.

26. See *Lumen Gentium* 12: "The holy people of God shares also in Christ's prophetic office; it spreads abroad a living witness to Him, especially by means of a life of faith and charity and by offering to God a sacrifice of praise, the tribute of lips which give praise to His name. The entire body of the faithful, anointed as they are by the Holy One, cannot err in matters of belief. They manifest this special property by means of the whole peoples' supernatural discernment in matters of faith when 'from the Bishops down to the last of the lay faithful' they show universal agreement in matters of faith and morals. That discernment in matters of faith is aroused and sustained by the Spirit of truth. It is exercised under the guidance of the sacred teaching authority, in faithful and respectful obedience to which the people of God accept that which is not just the word of men but truly the word of God. Through it, the people of God adhere unwaveringly to the faith given once and for all to the saints, penetrates it more deeply with right thinking, and applies it more fully in its life." See https://www.vatican.va.

27. The study, "The World of New Generations According to the Online Questionnaire," is available at http://secretariat.synod.va/content/synod2018/en/news/book--the-world-of-new-generations-according-to-the-online-quest.html.

28. "Final Document of the Synod of Bishops on Young People and Vocational Discernment" 13 (October 27, 2018), which received 221 votes in favor and 18 against, http://secretariat.synod.va.

29. "Final Document of the Synod of Bishops on Young People" 55, which received 209 votes in favor and 30 against.

30. "Final Document of the Synod of Bishops on Young People" 82. The beginning of Luke 8 notes that among Jesus's accompaniers were Mary Magdalene, Joanna, the wife of Chuza, Susanna, and many others who helped to support Jesus out of their own means.

31. "Final Document of the Synod of Bishops on Young People" 89.

32. See, for example, Mary Aquin O'Neill, "Toward a Renewed Anthropology," *Theological Studies* 36 (1975): 734–36, and the report "Women in Church and Society," Catholic Theological Society of America, 1978, 32.

33. Francis, Post-synodal Apostolic Exhortation *Christus Vivit* (March 25, 2019), no. 42, http://secretariat.synod.va.

34. "Final Document of the Synod of Bishops on Young People" 245, citing "Document of the Pre-synodal Meeting for the Preparation of the XV Ordinary Assembly of the Synod of Bishops," Rome (March 24, 2018), no. 12.

35. George Aschenbrenner, SJ, "Consciousness—Examen," *Review for Religious* 31 (1972): 14–21, available at https://www.ignatianspirituality.com/ignatian-prayer/the-examen/consciousness-examen/.

36. Eilish O'Gara, "Pope Francis Urges Young People to 'Make a Mess,'" *Newsweek* (July 14, 2015), https://www.newsweek.com; Francis visited Bolivia, Ecuador, and Paraguay from July 5 to 13, 2015.

37. Ruth is mentioned in *Christis Vivit* as exemplifying generosity toward her mother-in-law, no. 11, www.vatican.va.

38. R. M. W. Dixon and Alexandra Y. Aikhenvald, eds., *The Amazonian Languages*, Cambridge Language Surveys, (Cambridge: Cambridge University Press, 1999).

39. Cardinal Peter Turkson (b. 1948) from Ghana was the president of the Pontifical Council for Justice and Peace (2009–2017) and, until 2021, the prefect of the consolidated Dicastery for the Promotion of Integral Human Development. He presented the creation of REPAM in March 2015, https://zenit.org.

40. Amazon Synod, Final Document, "The Amazon: New Paths for the Church and for an Integral Ecology" (October 26, 2019), no. 103.

41. Francis appointed twelve scholars to the Pontifical Commission for the Study of the Diaconate of Women in August 2016. The commission met four times, completing its work in June 2018. Pope Francis gave the history portion of the report to the May 2019 meeting of UISG.

42. The new, ten-member commission included individuals competent to discuss contemporary diaconal ministry. Joshua J. McElwee, "Francis Creates New Women Deacons Commission, Naming Entirely New Membership," *National Catholic Reporter*, April 8, 2020, https://www.ncronline.org/news/theology/francis-creates-new-women-deacons-commission-naming-entirely-different-membership.

43. Conservative media appeared to support Tschugguel's theft and disposal of the statues, which were recovered by Italian authorities. Edward Pentin, "Austrian Catholic: Why I Threw Pachamama Statures into the Tiber," *National Catholic Register* (November 5, 2019), https://www.ncregister.com.

44. Even before Hummes landed in Rome, following his appointment, the Vatican issued a statement that the discipline of celibate clergy would not change. Following the publication of *Querida Amazonia*, Hummes stated that the Vatican would be taking up the question of ordaining married men, and his comments were seconded by Bishop Walmor Oliveira de Azevedo of the Diocese of Belo Horizonte, president of the National Conference of Bishops of Brazil. Edward Pentin, "Cardinal Hummes Pushes for Married Priests, and Lula Meets the Pope," *National Catholic Register* (February 13, 2020), https://www.ncregister.com.

45. Francis, Apostolic Letter *motu proprio, Spiritus Domini* (January 10, 2021), https://www.vatican.va.

46. Despite the proposed transparency of the synodal process, some episcopal conferences, including the USCCB, refused to share the names of nonparticipating dioceses.

47. Carol Glatz, "Synodal Process Showing Good Progress, Some Challenges, Vatican Says," *CNS* (February 7, 2022), cited in *Crux*, https://cruxnow.com.

48. Vatican News, "Synod of Bishops offers Initial Assessment of Synodal Process" (n.d.), https://www.vaticannews.va/en/vatican-city/news/2022-02/synod-bishops-synodality-first-stage-initial-assessment.html.

49. Secretary General of the Synod of Bishops. "*Vademecum* for the Synod on Synodality" (Vatican City, September 2021), https://www.usccb.org.

50. The U.S. Conference of Catholic Bishops divides the various dioceses and eparchies into fifteen regions across the United States. As many as 110 reports from independent groups were synthesized within the USCCB offices.

51. For example, Voice of the Faithful, the Boston-based group founded in the wake of sex-abuse scandals and consequent cover-ups, invited all comers to one of its 23 two-session Zoom events.

52. Synod of Bishops, XV Ordinary General Assembly, Final Document, "Young People, the Faith and Vocational Discernment" (October 27, 2018), no. 148.

53. Synod of Bishops, XV Ordinary General Assembly, Final Document, no. 121. The vote was 191 for, 51 against.

# 3. WOMEN AND THE CHURCH

1. Can. 129 §1. Those who have received sacred orders are qualified, according to the norm of the prescripts of the law, for the power of governance, which exists in the Church by divine institution and is also called the power of jurisdiction. §2. Lay members of the Christian faithful can cooperate in the exercise of this same power according to the norm of law.

2. Raffaella Petrini, FSE, Secretary General of the Governorate of the Vatican City State; Yvonne Reungoat, FMA, former Superior

General of the Daughters of Mary Help of Christian; Dr. Maria Lia Zervino, President of the World Union of Catholic Women's Organizations. Members of the Dicastery for Bishops receive dossiers to review and discuss at their twice-monthly meetings in Rome. Many members participate via Zoom, traveling to Rome more infrequently.

3. Canon 588 §2 requires a cleric (assumed to be a priest) to be the superior in mixed institutes and orders, but with the rescript, Pope Francis granted the Congregation for Institutes of Consecrated Life and Societies of Apostolic Life the right to derogate from the law on a case-by-case basis, https://press.vatican.va.

4. For example, on July 1, 2022, the Congregation of the Holy Cross elected Brother Paul Bednarczyk, CSC, as its superior general, and received Vatican approval three days later, https://international.la -croix.com.

5. *Costituzione Apostolica "Praedicate Evangelium" sulla Curia Romana e il suo servizio alla Chiesa e al Mondo, 19.03.2022* appeared on the ninth anniversary of Francis's accession to the See of Peter. The constitution has since been released in Arabic, English, Spanish, French, Italian, Polish, and Portuguese. See English edition, *Praedicate Evangelium* (March 19, 2022), www.vatican.va.

6. The Roman Curia, the administrative body of the papacy originated during the reign of Urban II, 1088–1099, and various commissions of cardinals developed over the years. In 1588, Sixtus V formalized its organization, which was successively revamped by Pius X (1908), Paul VI (1967), John Paul II (1988), and now Francis.

7. The former members are Francisco Javier Errázuriz Ossa, Archbishop-Emeritus of Santigo de Chile; Laurent Monsengwo Pasinya, Archbishop-Emeritus of Kinshasa; and George Pell, Prefect-Emeritus of the Secretariat for the Economy. Each belonged to the group from 2013 to 2018.

8. The Apostolic Constitution establishes a Pontifical Commission for the Protection of Minors within the Dicastery for the Doctrine of the Faith, see *Praedicate Evangelium* 78.

9. Kathleen Appler, DC; Simona Brambilla, ISMC; Maria Rita Calvo Sanz, ODN; Luigia Coccia, SMC; Olga Krizova, VDB; Françoise Massy, FMM; and Yvonne Reungoat, FMA.

10. From 2008 to 2018, Becquart headed the National Service for the Evangelization of Young People and for Vocations (SNEJV) within the Bishops' Conference of France (Conférence des évêques de France) (CEF).

11. Calduch-Benage was an expert at the 2008 Synod of Bishops of the Word of God and a member of the Pontifical Commission for the Study of the Diaconate of Women from 2016 to 2018.

12. From 2005 to 2021, Petrini was a staff member at the Congregation for the Evangelization of Peoples.

13. Cuda was named in 2022 as a member of the Pontifical Academy for Sciences and the Pontifical Academy for Life.

14. "Obituary, Sister Marjorie Keenan, R.S.H.M.," *Catholic New York* (November 4, 2016), https://www.cny.org.

15. Francis, *Praedicate Evangelium*, "Offices" 8.

16. Francis, *Praedicate Evangelium*, "Offices" 8.

17. *Lumen Gentium* 32, citing Rom 12:4–5; Eph 4–5; Gal 3:28; and Col 3:11.

18. Francis, Apostolic Letter *motu proprio, Ad Charisma Tuendum* (July 22, 2022), no. 4–5. Basically, assuming they are priests, they would be distinguished by their robes and use the title Reverend Monsignor, https://press.vatican.va. Interestingly, the Juris Doctor dissertation of Opus Dei founder Josemaría Escrivá is a study of authority and jurisdiction and is entitled *La Abadesa de las Huelgas: The Complete Works of Saint Josemaría Escrivá*, vol. 5 (Madrid: Rialp, 2016). First published in 1944.

19. Elizabeth McDonough, "Jurisdiction Exercised by Non-Ordained Members in Religious Institutes," *Canon Law Society of America Proceedings* 58 (1996): 292–307. Essentially, superiors have the authority to establish internal divisions and erect and suppress houses within their institutes, which they may represent; to admit, exclaustrate, release from temporary vows, and dismiss members (Canons 118, 581, 609, 616, 609, 634, 635, 638, 647, 656, 658, 686, 689, 699, as outlined

by McDonough, "Jurisdiction Exercised by Non-Ordained Members in Religious Institutes," 306).

20. McDonough, "Jurisdiction Exercised by Non-Ordained Members in Religious Institutes." Ratzinger was, at the time, Prefect of the Congregation for the Doctrine of the Faith, a position he held for 23 years, from 1982 to 2005, when he was elected Pope Benedict XVI. McDonough refers to Cardinal Ratzinger's *animadversiones* and suggested text of December 22, 1980, in *Congregatio Plenaria*, 294n4.

21. Frank Brennan, SJ, "Fr Frank's Homily–10 July 2022," https://catholicoutlook.org/fr-franks-homily-10-july-2022/.

22. The effort to derail the approval of women deacons appears to have been spearheaded by Sydney Archbishop Anthony Fisher, OP, successor to Cardinal George Pell. Christopher Lamb, "The Synod of Oz," *The Tablet* (July 23, 2022), 6–8.

23. Quoted in Geraldine Doogue, *Plenary Matters Podcast*, July 8, 2022, https://open.spotify.com/episode/1tGotFm5xVR4tKxhtBpiuf.

24. The question arises: Does the term *sacred orders*, here and elsewhere, refer only to priestly orders? Canon 1024 has been interpreted as restricting ordination as deacons and priests but stipulates "sacred orders" and is rooted in the codification of the *cursus honorem*, which denied diaconal ordination to anyone not destined for priesthood.

25. Other changes include modification to the way tribunal expenses are recovered by dioceses (sometimes subvention by bishops' conferences) and allows for a simpler process whereby a diocesan bishop can render a judgement.

26. Canon 1673 as amended by Francis maintains the requirement for a cleric as the head of a tribunal but allows the others to be laypersons. A sole clerical judge is permitted where strictly necessary. See Francis, Apostolic Letter *motu proprio Mitis Iudex Dominus Iesus* (August 15, 2015), www.vatican.va.

27. Joseph A. Komonchak, "A Smaller but Purer Church?," *Commonweal* (October 21, 2010), https://www.commonwealmagazine.org; see also Pope Emeritus Benedict XVI, "A Vision of the Future Church," https://www.madonnahouse.org.

28. David Gibson, "Archbishop Chaput Welcomes 'Smaller Church' of Holier Catholics," *Religion News Service* (October 21, 2016), https://www.ncronline.org.

29. Francis, "Opening Address of the XV Ordinary General Assembly of the Synod of Bishops" (September 3, 2018), www.vatican.va.

30. Richard R. Gaillardetz, "Towards a Contemporary Theology of the Diaconate," *Worship* 79, no. 5 (2005): 419–38.

31. Gaillardetz, citing John D. Zizioulas, *Being as Communion: Studies in Personhood and the Church* (Crestwood, NY: St. Vladimir's Seminary Press, 1985), 215–16.

32. Francis, "Opening Address of the XV Ordinary General Assembly of the Synod of Bishops" (September 3, 2018).

33. Louis Ellies Du Pin and W. Wotton, "Faustus, Bishop of Ries," in *A New History of Ecclesiastical Writers*, vol. 3, II (Farmington Hills, MI: Gale ECCO, 2018), 161.

34. In general, abbesses of these royal abbeys granted faculties for confessions, celebration of Eucharist, and preaching. They appointed parish priests and chaplains, granted dimissory letters, oversaw ecclesiastical and criminal cases, oversaw constitutions for religious houses, visited monasteries, and confirmed abbesses. Joan Morris, *The Lady Was a Bishop: The Hidden History of Women with Clerical Ordination and the Jurisdiction of Bishops* (New York: MacMillan Publishing Company, 1973); see also Joan Morris, "Women and Episcopal Power" *New Blackfriars* 53, no. 624 (1972): 205–10.

35. It is important to note that Mary MacKillop's excommunication was at least in part retribution for her complaining about a pederast priest. Jacqueline Maley, "MacKillop Exposed Paedophile Priest," *The Sydney Morning Herald* (September 25, 2020), https://www.smh.com.au.

36. See Ute E. Eisen, *Women Officeholders in Early Christianity: Epigraphical and Literary Studies*, trans. Linda M. Maloney (Collegeville, MN: Liturgical Press, 2000). Originally published as *Amtsträgerinnen im frühen Christentum: Epigraphische und literarische Studien* (Göttingen: Vandenhoeck & Ruprecht, 1996) and Kevin Madigan and

Carolyn Osiek, *Ordained Women in the Early Church: A Documentary History* (Baltimore: John's Hopkins University Press, 2011), among others.

37. Jean Morin, *Commentarius de sacris ecclesiae ordinationibus secundum antiquos et recentiores latinos, graecos, syros et babylonios in tres partes distinctus* (1655, 1695); (reprinted, Farnborough: Gregg, 1969).

38. Jean Pien, *Tractatus Praeliminaris De Ecclesiae Diaconissis*, in *Acta Sanctorum*, ed. J. Bollandus et al., vol. I (Antwerp: Bernard Albert Vander Plassch, 1746), i–xxviii.

39. Roger Gryson, *Le ministere des femmes dans l'Eglise ancienne*, Gembloux, Duculot, 1972 (*Recherches et syntheses*, Section d'histoire, IV); *The Ministry of Women in the Early Church* (Collegeville, MN: Liturgical Press) 1976; Philippe Delhaye, "Rétrospective et prospective des ministères féminins dans l'Eglise," *Revue théologique de Louvain* 3 (1972): 55–75; Cipriano Vagaggini, "L'ordinazione delle diaconesse nella tradizione greca e bizantina," *Orientalia Christiana Periodica* 40 (1974): 146–89; A.-G. Martimort, "A propos des ministères féminins dans l'Eglise," *Bulletin de littérature ecclésiastique* 74 (1973): 103–8; *Les Diaconesses: Essai historique* (Rome: Edizione Liturgiche, 1982).

40. Phyllis Zagano and Bernard Pottier, "Que savons-nous des femmes diacres?," *Laval théologique et philosophique* 74, no. 3 (2018): 437–45; trans. by the authors as "What Do We Know about Women Deacons?," *Asian Horizons* 13, no. 4 (2019): 647–58. See, for example, Gerhard L. Müller, *Priestertum und Diakonat. Der Empfänger des Weihesakramentes in schöpfungstheologischer und christologischer Perspektive*, Sammlung Horizonte NF 33 (Freiburg, 2000); Gerhard L. Muller, *Priesthood and Diaconate: The Recipient of the Sacrament of Holy Orders from the Perspective of Creation Theology and Christology*, trans. Michael J. Miller (San Francisco: Ignatius Press, 2002).

41. Phyllis Zagano, "A Tale of Two Deacons," *The Tablet* (September 4, 2021), 11.

42. At Vatican II, both Bishop Léon Bonaventura de Uriarte Bengoa, OFM (1891–1970) of Peru and Bishop Giuseppe Ruotolo (1898–1970) of Italy asked for the restoration of women to the diaconate; see *Acta et Documenta Concilio Oecumenico Vaticano II Apparando*;

Series I (*Antepraeparatoria*), *Typis Polyglottis Vaticanis*, 1960–61 (ADA-Indices), 11/11, 12/1.

43. *Lumen Gentium* 29, citing John 21:17 and Matthew 28:18ff.

44. *Lumen Gentium* 29.

45. For example, in 1970, there were 59,192 priests in the United States but 34,923 in 2021, with only two-thirds of those in active ministry; in the same period, there were 160,931 religious sisters but only 39,452 in 2021; and 11,623 religious brothers but only 3,832 in 2021. Concurrently, in 1970, the Catholic population in the United States grew from between 47.9 and 54.1 million in 1970 to between 66.8 and 73.2 million in 2021, depending on how the numbers were calculated. World data does not demonstrate such a severe drop in numbers of priests, but the numbers of religious in 2021 are roughly half of what they were in 1970, and the numbers of religious brothers and sisters demonstrate a steady decline. See Center for Applied Research in the Apostolate, "Frequently Requested Church Statistics," https://cara.georgetown.edu.

46. Francis, Apostolic Letter *Spiritus Domini* (January 15, 2021).

47. Francis, Apostolic Letter *Antiquum Minsterium* (May 10, 2021).

48. Francis, *Antiquum Minsterium*, quoting Paul VI, *Ministeria Quaedam*.

49. Sala Stampa della Santa Sede, *Bollettino* "Dichiarazione della Santa Sede" (July 21, 2022). When asked, Francis said the declaration should have been signed by the Secretary of State, https://press.vatican.va.

50. This section includes material from Phyllis Zagano, "Installed Lectors and Acolytes: Are Women Deacons Next?," *Pastoral Review* 17, no. 2 (2021): 11–16.

51. The Apostolic Library at the Vatican holds three from the East: Barberini gr. 336 (780), Vatican Manuscript gr. 1872 (1100), and the Codex Syriacus Vaticanus No. 19 (1550), and two from the West: Vatican Reginae lat. 337 (850) and the Ottobonianus lat. 313, Paris (850). The *Ordo ad diaconam faciendam* are deposited elsewhere, for example, from the East, the Bessarion Manuscript (1020) at the

monastery at Grotta Ferrata; the Coislin gr. 213 (1050) at the National Library in Paris. From the West, notably the Cambrai Manuscript 164 at the Cambrai Municipal Library (811); the Leofric Missal of Exeter at the Bodleian Library, Oxford (1050); and the *Ordo Romanus* of Hittorp, Cologne (850) and the Pontificals of St. Alban Abbey, Mainz (1030), the Abbey of Monte Cassino (1035), and Vallicella D5, Rome (1050), among others.

52. Francis, "Meeting with Bishops Taking Part in the World Meeting of Families," St. Charles Borromeo Seminary, Philadelphia (September 27, 2015), referring to Acts 6:1–15, www.vatican.va.

53. Joseph Ratzinger belonged to the First Quenquennium of the International Theological Commission, appointed May 1, 1969, and was reappointed the Second Quenquennium August 1, 1974, and was its president between 1981 and 2005, when he was elected Pope Benedict XVI. He resigned as pope in February 2013, to be followed by Jorge Mario Bergoglio, Pope Francis.

54. Sacred Congregation for the Doctrine of the Faith, Declaration, *Inter Insigniores*, "On the Question of Admission of Women to the Ministerial Priesthood" (October 15, 1976), www.vatican.va.

55. John Pau II, Apostolic Letter *Ordinatio Sacerdotalis* (Mary 22, 1994), www.vatican.va.

56. Congregation for the Doctrine of the Faith, *Responsum ad Propositum Dubium* Concerning the Teaching Contained in *"Ordinatio Sacerdotalis"* (October 28, 1995). This document was signed by Joseph Ratzinger, www.vatican.va.

57. Benedict XVI, Apostolic Letter *Omnium in Mentem* (October 26, 2009), www.vatican.va.

# 4. CONCLUSIONS

1. A gift from the people of Milan, the tiara was estimated at the time to be worth more than $80,000. Paul was reportedly greeted with shouts of *Viva il Papa povero* on leaving the basilica. Robert C. Doty,

"Pope Paul Donates His Jeweled Tiara to Poor of World," *New York Times* (November 14, 1964), 1.

2. Carl T. Mirbt, "The Vatican Council," in *Encyclopaedia Britannica*, ed. Hugh Chisholm, vol. 27, 11th ed. (London: Cambridge University Press, 1910–1911), 947–51.

3. Congregation for the Doctrine of the Faith, "Formula to Adopt from Now On in Cases in Which the Profession of Faith Is Prescribed by Law in Substitution of the Tridentine Formula and the Oath against Modernism, "*AAS* 59 (1967): 1058, www.vatican.va.

4. Vatican II, *Lumen Gentium* 32.

5. John Paul II, *Sollicitudo Rei Socialis* 49, citing Collect of the Mass "For the Development of Peoples": *Missale Romanum*, ed. typ. altera, 1975, 820.

6. The principle of "double effect" permits life-saving measures for the mother, such as in the case of cancer or the womb or an ectopic pregnancy.

7. Francis recently called "cancel culture" a "cultural fashion that levels everything out, makes everything equal and proves intolerant of differences." Loup Besmond de Senneville, "Francis Denounces 'Cancel Culture' during Canada Visit," *La Croix* (July 29, 2022), https://international.la-croix.com.

8. Catholic Leadership Institute, *Archdiocese of San Francisco Synodal Synthesis* (June 15, 2022), 10, https://sfarchdiocese.org.

9. See *Archdiocese of San Francisco Synodal Synthesis*, 4. Ordination of women, without distinguishing as deacons or as priests, was also given as example, https://www.sfarch.org/wp-content/uploads/2022/06/FINAL-Synodal-Synthesis-for-the-San-Francisco-Archdiocese.pdf.

10. Secretary General, Synod of Bishops, *Vademecum for the Synod on Synodality* (September 2021), appendix D, 3, https://www.usccb.org/resources/Vademecum-EN-A4.pdf.

11. For example, the dioceses of Buffalo, Louisville, Salt Lake City, and Trenton all mentioned these difficulties.

12. Diocese of Buffalo, *Listening in Love and Hope Synod Report* (June 2022), 3, https://www.buffalodiocese.org/synod/.

13. Malo Tresca, "Governance, Place of Women... France Drafts Its Synod Report," *La Croix* (June 16, 2022), https://international.la-croix.com.

14. Catholic Bishops' Conference of England and Wales, *National Synthesis Document* (June 22, 2022), no. 56, https://www.cbcew.org.uk/wp-content/uploads/sites/3/2022/06/synod-national-synthesis-england-wales.pdf.

15. Irish Catholic Bishops' Conference, Synthesis of the Consultation in Ireland for the Diocesan Stage of the Universal Synod 2021–2023 (2022).

16. Australia held Plenary Councils in 1885, 1895, 1905, and 1937, as well as Provincial Councils that included New Zealand in 1844 (Sydney) and 1869 (Melbourne), which primarily addressed matters of governance and jurisdiction.

17. Christopher Lamb, "Tensions Flare in Australia Council over Role of Women in Catholic Church," *The Tablet* (July 6, 2022), https://www.thetablet.co.uk.

18. Elise Ann Allen, "Vatican Says Germany's 'Synodal Path' Has No Power to Change Doctrine," *Crux* (July 21, 2022), https://cruxnow.com.

19. Nathalie Becquart, "Synodality: A Path of Personal and Communal Conversion," *The Way* 61, no. 3 (2022): 63–70.

20. Gerard O'Connell, "Pope Francis Responds to Attacks from EWTN, Other Church Critics: 'They Are the Work of the Devil,'" *America* (September 21, 2021), https://www.americamagazine.org.

21. EWTN states that it reaches 250 million people in 140 countries though eleven networks. It also has a 24-hour radio network that reaches approximately 350 radio stations across the United States.

22. "Catholic News Service to Cease Domestic Operations at Year's End," Catholic News Service (May 4, 2022), https://catholicnews.com/catholic-news-service-to-cease-domestic-operations-at-years-end/; Carol Zimmermann, "Our Sunday Visitor announces launch of new Catholic news service in 2023" Catholic News Service (July 7, 2022).

23. Phil Lawler, "The Pope's Stalled Vatican Reforms" *Catholic Culture* (January 5, 2022), https://www.catholicculture.org.

24. Pope John Paul II renovated Vatican buildings to create the monastery, which housed successive groups of contemplative nuns invited there to pray for the pope. Following the five-year tenures of nuns from the Order of St. Clare, Discalced Carmelites, and Benedictines that began in 1994, the Visitandine nuns were asked to leave toward the end of 2012, when renovations began on the building.

25. Once Benedict retired, he stopped wearing the *pellegrina*, which some see as a symbol of office. However, he continued to wear a white cassock. He is perhaps more properly known as the bishop emeritus of Rome.

26. Francis, "Address of His Holiness Pope Francis to the International Union of Superiors General" (May 12, 2016), www.vatican.va.

27. Antonio Spadaro, "A Big Heart Open to God: An Interview with Pope Francis," *America* (September 30, 2013), https://www.americamagazine.org; Joshua J. McElwee, "Pope Calls Again for 'Incisive' Women's Presence in Church, Offers No Specifics," *National Catholic Reporter* (February 7, 2015), www.vatican.va; Loup Besmond de Senneville, "The Pope Urges 'A More Incisive Female Presence in the Church,'" *La Croix*, (October 9, 2020), https://international.la-croix.com. *America* originally edited parts of Francis's comments and translated "more incisive" as "stronger."

28. "Introductory Remarks by His Holiness Pope Francis," Synod for the Family 2015 (October 5, 2015), www.vatican.va.